To My Friend Ron
With Blessings!

Dave & Judy
2010
May

Henri Nouwen: His Life and Vision

(Photo by Ron van den Bosch, used with permission)

HENRI NOUWEN
HIS LIFE AND VISION

Michael O'Laughlin

NOVALIS

DARTON·LONGMAN+TODD

ORBIS BOOKS

Maryknoll, New York 10545

Founded in 1970, Orbis Books endeavors to publish works that enlighten the mind, nourish the spirit, and challenge the conscience. The publishing arm of the Maryknoll Fathers and Brothers, Orbis seeks to explore the global dimensions of the Christian faith and mission, to invite dialogue with diverse cultures and religious traditions, and to serve the cause of reconciliation and peace. The books published reflect the views of their authors and do not represent the official position of the Maryknoll Society. To learn more about Maryknoll and Orbis Books, please visit our website at www.maryknoll.org.

Published in 2005 by Orbis Books, Maryknoll, New York 10545-0308.

Published in Great Britain in 2005 by Darton, Longman and Todd Ltd, 1 Spencer Court, 140-142 Wandsworth High Street, London SW18 4JJ.

Published in Canada in 2005 by Novalis, Saint Paul University, 223 Main Street, Ottawa, Ontario K1S 1C4.

Grateful acknowledgment is made to the following publishers for permission to reprint material from books by Henri Nouwen: Doubleday, a division of Random House, Inc., for *Reaching Out,* copyright © 1975 by Henri J.M. Nouwen; *The Road to Daybreak,* copyright © 1988 by Henri J.M. Nouwen; *A Cry for Mercy,* copyright © 1981 by Henri J.M. Nouwen; *The Inner Voice of Love,* copyright © 1996 by Henri J.M. Nouwen. Crossroad Publishing, for *Sabbatical Journey,* copyright © 1998 by the Estate of Henri J.M. Nouwen; *In the Name of Jesus,* copyright ©1993 by Henri J.M. Nouwen; *Life of the Beloved,* copyright © 1992 by Henri J.M. Nouwen; *Here and Now,* copyright © 1994 by Henri J.M. Nouwen. Ave Maria Press, for *Can You Drink the Cup?* copyright © 1996 by Ave Maria Press. HarperCollins Publishers for *Intimacy,* copyright © 1969 by Henri J.M. Nouwen; *Letters to Marc about Jesus,* copyright © 1988 by Henri J.M. Nouwen; *Bread for the Journey,* copyright © 1997 by Henri J.M. Nouwen; *Our Greatest Gift,* copyright © 1994 by Henri J.M. Nouwen.

Thanks to all who granted permission to use their photographs in this book. We apologize for any credits that were omitted; these can be corrected in a future reprint.

Learn more about Nouwen, his writing and the work of the Henri Nouwen Society. Visit www.HenriNouwen.org

Queries regarding rights and permissions should be addressed to:
Orbis Books, P.O. Box 308, Maryknoll, NY 10545-0308.

Manufactured in the United States of America.

Designed by Roberta Savage.

Library of Congress Cataloging-in-Publication Data: 2005016720
Orbis ISBN 1-57075-612-0

A catalogue record for this book is available from the British Library.
DLT ISBN 0 232 52633 8

Library and Archives Canada Cataloguing in Publication Data:
A catalogue record for this book is available from Library and Archives Canada
Novalis ISBN 2-89507-710-X

To Marta, Andy, and Nick—

I am blessed to have you as companions on my journey!

Contents

Acknowledgments

I would like to thank several people who helped bring this book out looking better than anything I could have done without their assistance: first of all, thanks to Gabrielle Earnshaw, the archivist of the Henri Nouwen Archives at the University of St. Michael's College. In response to a query from me Gabrielle undertook a research project to clarify the course of Nouwen's university career. I would also like to thank Louis ter Steeg, Sue Mosteller, and Peter Weiskel for reading all or parts of the manuscript, making corrections, and offering me great advice.

I must also give a lot of credit to my editor, Robert Ellsberg, who saw the need for a book like this one and also took up the job of chief photo editor. He and the staff at Orbis Books, particularly Roberta Savage, deserve a great deal of recognition for the exemplary style and look of this book. Laurent Nouwen and Jim Forest both helped assemble some of the pictures used from the Nouwen family photo collection. Gabrielle Earnshaw of the Henri Nouwen Archives and Maureen Wright at the Henri Nouwen Literary Centre also worked on assembling the photos you see here. Many other friends of Henri Nouwen were extremely generous in sharing their personal photographs. Thanks to everyone for all your help!

(Photo by Todd Rothrock. Courtesy Photograph Series, Henri Nouwen Archives)

Introduction

Many, many people consider Henri Nouwen their favorite spiritual author, and few writers of spiritual books have so many enthusiastic readers. Through his more than fifty books Nouwen touched thousands of people around the world with his compelling interpretation of Christian faith and the Christian gospel. His refreshing approach was not derived from any new psychological or philosophical theory; instead it was simply based on who he was himself and the efforts he made to find God. His authority as a spiritual writer was based on the fact that he spoke from the heart, and he had a gift, maybe even a "charism" to see spiritual things in very clear terms and to communicate what he was feeling to others in a caring, profound, yet simple way. It is not unusual to read something by Henri Nouwen and to feel like the gospel is starting to make sense for the first time, or that Henri Nouwen somehow knew what you have always thought or felt in your heart, but never heard anyone say. Henri truly had a gift for reaching people, and his message was deeply Christian.

However, the most wonderful thing about Henri Nouwen is that he was not "just" a writer. He was someone who was really living the message that he was preaching, and hearing his life story is like reading one of his books—it feels inspiring and challenging to think that another very ordinary person, just like any of us, could try so hard to find God and enrich so many lives in the process. Henri Nouwen was an example of how to be a real Christian.

I knew Henri personally. I was his teaching assistant when he taught at Harvard University. We stayed in touch after we

Henri with clown, 1972.
(Photo by Ron van den Bosch, used with permission)

both left Harvard, and eventually he became like a spiritual father to me. As our relationship deepened, I became much more interested in who Henri was and how he was able to live as he did; I thought that everything about his life could be like a teaching for me. I always believed that the best teachers could teach without words, just by their living example, and in this regard Henri did not disappoint me; he was that kind of teacher.

Nor was I his only student. There are thousands of people who have learned something essential to their lives from Henri Nouwen. Just last week someone told me that Henri's *Life of the Beloved* was one of the five most important books she ever read, and people say things like that to me all the time. This book is written for all the people who have read Nouwen's books and have the same feeling, that Henri Nouwen touched them with his writing and his message of God's love. Maybe you are one of those readers, and now you want to know more about Henri himself, like I did. If you are curious about who this inspirational author was or would like to know how he lived his life, then this book is for you.

Like the books that Henri wrote, this book is not too long, and I have also tried to make it fairly readable. The illustrations include many photos that have never been published previously. I hope that those readers who value an author's efforts to live out what he teaches to others will find this book interesting and even helpful.

(Photo by Mary Carney, used with permission)

What I intend to do in the following pages is to lay out the ups and downs and main events that made up Henri's life. It is common practice in the l'Arche community, which Henri joined in 1986, to make a "life story book" that contains photos and testimonials celebrating who we are and the life that we are given. I don't know if Henri ever created his own life story book or not, but it has been a wonderful experience for me to make a life story book for him. Henri taught that everyone's life matters, and after reading the following pages, I think that you will see why he made this one of the central themes of his message.

There are many aspects of Henri's life that I am leaving out of this short presentation, but one of these omissions is the most glaring: Henri was a great friend to thousands of people. He spent hours every day on the telephone and at his desk writing letters to people. His schedule was filled with appointments and trips to see his many friends and to make new ones. Henri also kept in close touch with his family throughout his life. Although I do mention a few people who played a unique and visible role in Henri's life, I have not found it possible to include more than a handful of references to the hundreds of important relationships, visits, and encounters that Henri had with his family, his friends, and people everywhere. So, let me apologize in advance to the many people whose deep relationship with Henri formed another important chapter of his life, but who are not mentioned here.

Henri (on the right) and his brother Paul with their grandparents.
(Nouwen family albums)

A Low Land by the Sea

Henri Nouwen came from the small, maritime country we know as Holland, or the Netherlands. The words "Holland" and "Netherlands" both mean "low country." Holland is indeed mostly low land bordered by the sea. We are all familiar with the traditional images of Holland—the windmills, the wooden shoes, the dykes, and the tulips—but what was it really like for Henri Nouwen to grow up there?

Henri was born in 1932 in a small city called Nijkerk. He was the oldest of four children. His father worked for the government, in the tax department, and Henri's grandfather was the clerk of another nearby town. You could say that in this small-town Dutch world, the Nouwens were a prominent family. They were cultured, well-educated people with good jobs and a certain intellectual flair.

Holland is much changed today, but before World War II, and even for some time after the war, it was strictly divided into different communities. The basis of the division was not race, as it is in some parts of the world, but religion. The Dutch religious communities did not mix, but kept strictly to themselves. Catholics were not as numerous as Protestants, but they made up for being a minority by expressing their Catholicism in everything they did. To maintain their separate identity they only read Catholic papers, listened to Catholic radio, patronized Catholic restaurants and businesses, and they tried to stay clear of anything that did not come from a recognized Catholic source. This voluntary separation was in agreement with Catholic policy at the time, and the church hierarchy approved of the voluntary segregation of the Catholic population in

Henri held by his mother, Maria Ramselaar Nouwen.
(Nouwen family albums)

(Photo by Jim Forest, used with permission)

"My first twenty-four years of life were basically years to prepare myself for the Catholic priesthood. I was born and raised in a Roman Catholic family, went to Roman Catholic schools, and lived a life in which I related exclusively to Roman Catholics. It was a time in which all boundaries were clear."

—The Road to Peace

Holland. Dutch Catholics lived in a separate realm under the auspices of their church. Dutch Catholics were much more insulated against the rest of society than were Catholics in any other country, and Dutch Catholics were recognized everywhere as being extremely pious and very observant. The Vatican considered the Dutch to be a model church.

Thus, the community in which Henri Nouwen was born and grew up was very sheltered and very Catholic. Within this world he received a great deal of affirmation and support. Henri had an uncle who was a priest and an aunt who was a nun, and he decided early on to follow in their footsteps. Because he was inclined toward religion and the priesthood, he was kept even more within bounds than might have been the case otherwise. His was a protected world that did not allow him to meet persons different from himself or even form an opinion about many of the problems of society. Thinking back to his youth and the day he was ordained, Henri had these thoughts:

On that 21st day of July, 1957, when my life-long dream to become a priest was realized, I was a very naive twenty-five-year-old. My life had been well-protected. I had grown up as in a beautifully kept garden surrounded by thick hedges. It was a garden of loving parental care, innocent boy scout experiences, daily mass and communion, long hours of study with very patient teachers, and many years of happy but very isolated seminary life. I came out of it all full of love for Jesus, and full of desire to bring the Gospel to the world but without being fully aware that not everybody was waiting for me. I had only met—and that quite cautiously—a few Protestants, had never encountered an unbeliever, and certainly had no idea about other religions. Divorced people were unknown to me, and if there were any priests who had left the priesthood, they were kept away from me. The greatest "scandal" I had experienced was a friend leaving the seminary! [1]

Henri and his mother.
(Nouwen family albums)

So, Henri's first experiences as a boy and a young man in the land of his birth were of an ordered, close knit, and very religious community. Although his family was educated and prosperous, Henri himself felt that he reached adulthood without having really seen or understood the world. He grew up in "a beautifully kept garden surrounded by thick hedges." This was not so much due to his family's attitude as it was due to the strong religious attitudes and barriers in Dutch society at that time. Dutch Catholics had no dealings with outsiders, and everyone lived within a small circle of family friends and acquaintances. This stable but sheltered background would be an important factor in Nouwen's later life, providing him with a fixed point of reference and a strong sense of identity, but also a sense that he needed to get beyond the protective hedges of his childhood to really experience life.

Henri (seated), with his brother Paul, their parents, Laurent and Maria Nouwen, and maternal grandparents. (Nouwen family albums)

Family

Relationships, especially family relationships, were always of paramount importance in Henri Nouwen's life. He thrived on interaction and cared deeply for his parents, his brothers, and his sister. He was known, in the family circle and to his friends, not by his given name, "Henri," but by a more Dutch-sounding equivalent, "Harrie." His brothers were named Paul and Laurent, like his father, and his sister's name was Laurien. The Nouwens were a happy family, with Henri himself being the only possible exception. Despite his normal upbringing and consistent achievements, he was a

Henri (right) with his parents, brother Paul, and young sister, Laurien.
(Nouwen family albums)

Henri at eight. (Nouwen family albums)

"I had grown up in a beautifully kept garden surrounded by thick hedges. It was a garden of loving parental care, innocent boy scout experiences, daily mass and communion, long hours of study with very patient teachers. . . . I came out of it all full of love for Jesus and full of desire to bring the Gospel to the world."

—Can You Drink the Cup?

somewhat sensitive, insecure boy, quick to pick up on any negative vibrations or subtle conflicts he sensed around him. Because of this underlying sense of anxiety, we cannot say that all of Henri's memories or feelings about his family were pleasant and unclouded.

Even though he was the oldest child and received a lot of attention and support, he was never free of feelings of uncertainty and even shame. Henri was a smart boy and possessed excellent social skills, but he was terribly uncoordinated and clumsy. This made it hard for him to participate in sports. He was also troubled by doubts that maybe his parents did not really care for him; maybe things were not as nice as they seemed, or maybe he did not measure up. Here is one of Henri's memories of this sort of feeling:

When I was a small child I kept asking my father and mother: "Do you love me?" I asked that question so often and so persistently that it became a source of irritation to my parents. Even though they assured me hundreds of times that they loved me I never seemed fully satisfied with their answers and kept on asking the same question. [2]

In Henri's own evaluation of the family dynamic, his father and mother voiced equally influential, but different, positions. His father was proud of his independence and of being a self-made man. He urged his sons to make their way in the world, and to make it on their own. His mother's gentler counsel was for Henri to always remember to stay close to God and to remember that he was loved for who he was, regardless of his success or failure. In Henri's estimation, the voices of his parents were hard to reconcile. Which one was right? Probably the dichotomy was not as clear as it later seemed to Henri, but this point would trouble Henri for much of his lifetime.

It can be said, without fear of contradiction, that Henri felt more accepted by his mother and felt closer to her than he did to anyone else. As a sensitive person, Henri needed affection and acceptance. His father loved him but seemed to have standards that Henri could never meet. Throughout his life Henri yearned to find the same sense of acceptance and engagement he felt with his mother from his very accomplished and energetic father. Henri was a restless, idealistic person, someone not easily satisfied, and perhaps he longed for more from his father than he could reasonably have given him.

Although this undercurrent was always a factor in his life, Henri was not an unhappy child. He absorbed the security and stimulation of a wonderful childhood home. He enjoyed his family and was able to do so many great things later in life because of the love he received as a boy. The atmosphere in the Nouwen home was progressive and orderly. For his part, Henri's father was an articulate intellectual. He was always pondering and discussing the great topics of the day. Henri's mother was fond of writing and literature. She read widely in several European languages. Together they created an intellectual ambience that provided endless stimulation for the young Henri Nouwen.

Henri, Paul, and their parents.
(Nouwen family albums)

Of course, religion was another major component in the family's makeup. Catholic piety and purpose were important for the entire community in which Henri grew up, and at home Catholicism was practiced on a daily basis. Within this very religious family, Henri's maternal grandmother was especially devout and had a special role, that of promoting and encouraging spirituality and devotion. Her son, Fr. Anton the priest, was a frequent visitor to the Nouwen house and was a natural role model for Henri.

Understanding Henri's family is one key to understanding Henri Nouwen. In Henri's family we see dedication to religion and spirituality, balanced within a caring, educated, and cultured lifestyle. He inherited from his father an energetic sense of purpose and drive. From his mother came his great concern for others and his tenderness. This family was a strong one, capable of properly nurturing and then sending someone like Henri Nouwen into the world.

Henri playing priest in his attic "chapel." (Nouwen family albums)

Child Priest

Henri was sure that he wanted to be a priest by the time he was five years old. His family was quite pious, and the society in which he lived was centered around their religious confession, so perhaps this early interest in the priesthood is not at all surprising. Many young boys in Catholic homes considered becoming priests. However, Henri's desire was manifest early and never wavered. He did not go through a phase later when he wanted to be a fireman or an explorer; he remained focused on the priesthood. His mother and father supported his vocation, if that was what it was, and so did his maternal grandmother. By the time Henri was eight he had persuaded his family to allow him to set up his own chapel in the attic, and his grandmother provided Henri with some of the essential items he needed to create a "real" Catholic service. She owned a department store and had a carpenter and a seamstress who both did work for her, so she had a miniature altar built and vestments made, and she bought Henri a paten and chalice. Thus at eight Henri began to officiate at his own family chapel, before friends and relatives, often with his brother Paul acting as his attendant. He bestowed blessings, named those whom he favored to a hierarchy all his own, and addressed sermons and admonitions to the household and family friends.

What are we to make of this early fascination with the church and the priesthood? Henri had little aptitude for sports or games involving physical prowess, so perhaps this was one reason he was drawn very early to embrace the religious life of his family and his community. However, there could be a deeper aspect to Henri's fascination with the mass. James Hillman,

(Nouwen family albums)

the American psychologist, has theorized that persons with clear charismatic gifts, those unique people who often make a considerable impact on society through politics, acting, literature, or entertainment, show an early predilection for their later life's work. Henri Nouwen certainly fits Hillman's model: at a very early stage in his life he gravitated almost magnetically towards his calling or mission.

One of Henri's friends, Robert Jonas, believes that what drew Henri into his boy-priest fantasy was his fascination with the Eucharist. Besides the writing of spiritual books, the Eucharist was to be his passion and his life's work, a holy ritual in which he would stand in communion with the world and with God. If the Eucharist was destined to become the bedrock of his existence, is it really surprising that as soon as Henri was able to make any sort of choice he would decide to be a priest, and as soon as he was able to act out his feelings he would begin to officiate at his little altar in the family attic?

"Since I was six years old, I had felt a great desire to be a priest. . . . By the time I was eight years old, I had converted the attic of our home to a children's chapel, where I played Mass, gave sermons to my parents and relatives, and set up a whole hierarchy with bishops, priests, deacons and altar servers among my friends."

—Can You Drink the Cup?

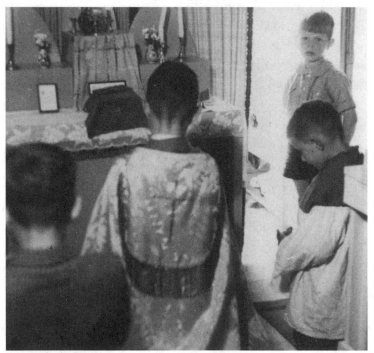

(Nouwen family albums)

World War II

When Henri was eight years old, Holland was invaded by the German army. Even though his parents made great efforts to shelter their children from the harsh realities of the conflict raging around them, the war and the German occupation made a deep impression on Henri Nouwen. Not only were the Germans engaged in a systematic roundup of Jews and anyone else considered an enemy of the Third Reich, they imposed rationing and many other harsh conditions on the Dutch populace.

Many years later Henri would recall with lingering horror the privations of the Hunger Year, and any visit he would make to Germany filled him with feelings of ambivalence. Henri's mother spoke German fluently and was able to avoid trouble with the occupiers, but Henri's father needed to stay completely out of sight to keep from being sent to a work camp. He constructed a hiding place for himself in a section of a wall of the house beneath a window sill, and he spent many hours there reading. Luckily, on the day when the house was searched, he was in the hidden compartment and was not discovered.

Although Henri's life and the life of his family were impacted in many ways by the war and by German occupation, the conflict also led to some positive developments. The Dutch bishops acted courageously in comparison with the bishops of other Nazi-occupied countries. Encouraged by the bishops, the great majority of Catholics withheld their support from the Germans. The occupation fostered solidarity not only among Catholics, but nationwide. The Dutch bishops, togeth-

(Courtesy The Netherlands Institute for War Documentation)

er with their Protestant counterparts, denounced every misdeed of the Nazis, especially the deportation of the Jews. This national solidarity against tyranny during the war was very important to the changing sense of Dutch identity.

Another positive development was this: in many occupied European countries Catholic priests and Christian activists were placed in work and concentration camps, which led to a breakdown of the traditional divisions in society: Priests were forced to work alongside and make common cause with laypeople. Dutch Catholics found that they were able to talk to and work with Protestants and socialists. Although the war was a traumatic event of massive proportions that shook Europe to the core, the successful defeat of the Nazis, plus the breakdown of traditional boundaries and age-old structures that occurred as a result of the war, particularly in Holland, opened the door to a series of changes in the Catholic Church.

German troops enter Amsterdam in 1940. (Courtesy The Netherlands Institute for War Documentation)

Henri with his mother and brother Paul. (Nouwen family albums)

"The Second World War had come to a very critical stage, but my parents were able to keep me and my brother away from the cruelties of war and even provided us with a rather regular school life."
—Can You Drink the Cup?

These changes would directly impact the life and training of Henri Nouwen.

By the time he was twelve, young Henri had made up his mind to leave home and enter the minor seminary. For Catholic boys interested in pursuing a vocation to the priesthood, a commitment to the seminary at such a young age was not unusual in that period. Henri's family was unwilling to consider his entering the seminary then, however, because of

*"How strange that
this cruel war was the
context of my vocation to
the priesthood. . . . Our
parents taught us
something about God
that is hard to teach to
a generation with no
memories of bomb
shelters, the destruction of
large cities like Rotterdam
and London, and the
constant fear of death."*
—The Road to Daybreak

(Nouwen family albums)

(Nouwen family albums)

the quickly changing military situation. The Allies were engaging the Germans on both the eastern and western fronts and advancing towards Berlin. Instead of seminary, Henri was sent to the local gymnasium, which is the equivalent of an American or British prep school in the German- and Dutch-speaking countries of Europe. When the war came to an end, his family moved to The Hague, and there Henri finished his secondary schooling in a Catholic college run by the Jesuits.

The Dutch church had been fundamentally altered by its wartime experience of resistance to German tyranny and national solidarity. Henri Nouwen came of age as part of a postwar generation that realized that everything would need to be rebuilt and many changes in society would result. This generation would bring about dramatic changes in Catholicism, not only in Holland, but around the world.

Seminary

It was only at the age of eighteen that Henri was finally able to enter the minor seminary, there joining other boys his age for a final year of studies. By this point his uncle Anton had been made a monsignor and put in charge of this same minor seminary, so Henri's transition there was made much smoother. In a way, because his uncle was the rector of the school, he remained within the family orbit even after he opted for the separate and secluded life of a seminarian.

The major seminary at Rijsenburg, where Henri studied theology. (Archdiocese of Utrecht. Courtesy Maria ter Steeg)

At this point Henri must have felt that his life was finally under way. The war was over, and he was able to pursue his priestly studies after a very long wait. The following year Henri matriculated to the "major" or higher seminary. His standing among the other seminary students, despite his relatively late entrance in the program, was meteoric. As a young man Henri was extremely hard-working, pious, and likeable. The fact that

Chapel of the Philosophicum Dijnselburg where Henri studied before entering Rijsenburg Seminary. (Archdiocese of Utrecht. Courtesy Maria ter Steeg)

he was the nephew of the minor seminary's rector also counted in his favor, and Henri thus enjoyed a double prominence. He was eventually elected to be the "senior," or class representative, so it was Henri who rose to speak for his classmates in assemblies and before visitors. His public speaking career was off to an early start.

Henri's seminary experience was in many ways similar to that of Catholic seminarians everywhere during that period. He spent long hours studying, going to class, and attending daily mass and other prayer services at fixed points during the day. There was always work to be done, and any number of services anchored to the yearly liturgy of feast days. There was little time for idleness. Henri was assigned to work in the library, and he himself created a Newman Society chapter.

One of the strong underlying themes of Catholic seminary life was the formation of an intelligent, obedient priestly individual who could maintain a sober attitude and keep his emotions and his body in check. Students were allowed three visits home per year, and were strongly discouraged from forming any special friendships.

For Henri Nouwen, and for all seminarians, training for a

life of solitude and celibacy began in earnest in the major seminary, and was built on a foundation of negative attitudes toward the body that were as old as Christianity. Although his seminary experience was not as strict as that of many other priests, Henri Nouwen was provided a strong, traditional orientation toward (or one might say "against") sexual matters. This antierotic element was only one aspect of a complete program of formation that was designed to mold the seminarian into a disciplined and articulate spokesperson ready and able to serve his community and his bishop.

There have been many priests and former priests who have criticized or condemned their program of training for both its harshness and lack of understanding of human nature. Interestingly enough, Henri Nouwen never offered any such negative assessments of his own seminary experience. He apparently enjoyed his time as a seminarian, and regarded the discipline he learned there in positive terms. In one conversation much later in life Henri's attitude to his training surprised his friends, who at the time were laughing over a 1940s sex-

"I lived in the same large building for six years. The discipline was strict, the lifestyle simple and solid, the teaching very traditional and conservative. I could only leave the building in the company of others. My great contribution to the 'liberation' of the seminary was bicycles. I convinced the staff that having bikes was good for seminarians."
—Sabbatical Journey

Henri with his mother, his Uncle Tennis Ramselaar, and his Uncle Anton, a priest who played a major role in his life.
(Nouwen family albums)

Henri with fellow seminarians in the library. (Nouwen family albums)

education manual for children. Nouwen protested that that was how he had been trained, too: "That's what it was like for us in the seminary," he protested. "You don't know what it was like."[3] Henri recalls seminary as a wholesome, if isolating, experience. He himself was probably close to what he later styled as the typical seminarian:

> *It is not too long ago that the stereotype of the seminarian offered the picture of a very nice, sweet boy, somewhat talkative, easily excited about such innocent things as a recent article, naïve, inexperienced especially in matters of sex, but always good-natured, friendly, smiling, and ready to help even when not asked.*[4]

As someone with a deep love for God and a natural gregariousness and need to succeed, he was almost ideal seminary material. He is remembered with admiration both by his teachers and the other seminarians. Although he certainly distinguished himself at his seminary studies, looking back, he did not credit this to aptitude or intelligence on his part, so much as extremely hard work.

Dutch Theology

Catholic doctrines can often seem old-fashioned or slow to change, especially in contrast to the more modern or flexible teachings of some Protestant churches. However, the Catholic Church has occasionally undergone tremendous change in a short time, and that was the case in Holland in the period in which Henri Nouwen came of age. In fact, it would be difficult to name another country where the evolution of Catholic theology was as dramatic as it was in the Netherlands after World War II.

The Holland of Henri Nouwen's youth was a tidy, conservative country, characterized by a strict and long-established separation between Catholics and all other religious groups. Safe within their enclave, the Catholics of Holland were considered the most observant and loyal of any Catholics in Europe. It was a self-sufficient, not to say isolated, community. Dutch Catholics had their own separate society, and there was a strong sense of group identity.

(Courtesy The Netherlands Institute for War Documentation)

This insular, sealed-off existence was severely compromised when Holland was invaded by the Nazis. As mentioned previously, many Dutch Catholics were put into work or concentration camps, and some were even killed. The Dutch Catholics placed in camps experienced a real breakdown in their separatist mentality; they suddenly found themselves thrust into close contact with the other types of Dutchmen that they had been avoiding all their lives, and they discovered that they had much more in common with them than they could ever have imagined. Both in and out of the camps these various types of Hollanders also united in resisting a common

Henri with children at their first
Holy Communion.
(Nouwen family albums)

enemy, the German occupiers.

The social impact of the Nazi invasion on Holland was
truly enormous. German occupation traumatized the Dutch
with regard to all forms of despotism, real or imagined. Once
the Germans were defeated and the traditional institutions of
Dutch society began to reassert themselves, Dutch Catholicism
suddenly found itself at a crossroads. Many loyal believers were
no longer willing to tolerate the top-down structure of traditional Catholicism. Everyone realized that the rebuilding of
Europe called less for obedience than for creative thinking.

In Holland, more than in many other countries, change
was in the air. Dialogues and experimentation began to take
place at all levels of the Catholic Church and between

Catholic and many non-Catholic entities. New thinking and experimental ecclesiastical reforms, some of which had been discussed for over a decade by theologians and clergy in French-speaking Europe, were taken up enthusiastically and actually implemented in Holland. These changes were so dramatic that travel agents in France began arranging tours to the Netherlands, not to see the tulips, but to see "the new Catholicism."

As a seminarian and a young Dutch priest Henri Nouwen participated directly in the transformation of Dutch theology and practice. In his seminary classes he saw the new questions and new answers first begin to impact traditional priestly training. After he was ordained, he had a chance to step into the vanguard of the changes sweeping the church. There was a desire to rediscover the Bible, reform the liturgy, replace medieval observances and rituals with more Christ-centered ones, and make new knowledge from the fields of philosophy and psychology part of Catholic thinking. Henri Nouwen's approach to spiritual questions and to theology later in life was deeply influenced by his participation in this sudden evolution of Dutch theology. He quickly grasped that knowing Jesus and coming to greater personal self-awareness was much more central to a healthy, faithful life than observance of the traditional liturgical calendar or the previous overriding interest among Catholics in orthodoxy, obedience, and self-denial. As he emerged as a gifted young priest with strong writing and speaking abilities, he brought to others a message that was fully in line with the flowering of Dutch theology taking place all around him.

"In every phase of my search I've discovered . . . that Jesus Christ stands at the center of my seeking. If you were to ask me point-blank, 'What does it mean to you to live spiritually?' I would have to reply, 'Living with Jesus at the center.'"

—Letters to Marc about Jesus

Cardinal Alfrink

Cardinal Bernard Alfrink,
the bishop of Utrecht.
(Nouwen family albums)

"Bernard Alfrink, the Cardinal Archbishop of the Netherlands, laid his hands on my head, dressed me with a white chasuble, and offered me his golden chalice to touch with my hands bound with a linen cloth. Thus I was ordained to the priesthood. . . . I will never forget the deep emotions that stirred my heart at that moment."

—Can You Drink the Cup?

One of the most significant figures in the life of Henri Nouwen was his bishop. Bernard Cardinal Alfrink was a biblical scholar. He was a professor on the faculty of Nijmegen University for many years before being transferred to work in the episcopal chancery. Alfrink was an enthusiastic, dedicated scholar, and even after he was made bishop of Utrecht in 1955 he continued to publish articles on the Bible. His life was also one of considerable adaptation and evolution. Despite his later reputation as a liberal churchman, Cardinal Alfrink held very traditional views when he assumed office, as can be seen by his early pronouncements. However, Cardinal Alfrink came to the point of allowing many sweeping changes, once he became caught up in the extraordinary series of events that led to the theological "Prague Spring" that took place in the Dutch church in the fifties and sixties.

Alfrink's profound interest in the Bible influenced his views regarding church polity. He found in the apostolic period of early Christianity a model of collegiality that he thought very pertinent to Catholicism in the modern world. Instead of a top-down authoritarian model, he encouraged a new level of collegial cooperation and consultation among the bishops of Holland. Cardinal Alfrink also created a national pastoral council that gave laypeople a voice in the church for the first time.

In the postwar era, "dialogue" became the watchword of the Dutch effort to include previously excluded parties in the decision-making process, and Cardinal Alfrink allowed a myriad of dialogues and consultations to go on. Holland is in many ways a consensus-seeking society, and the extraordinary number of dialogues and consultations occurring in and around the Catholic Church at that time were very much in character for Dutch society. Everyone was seeking consensus, and everyone was consulted!

It was in this period that Henri finished his seminary studies and was ordained by Archbishop Alfrink. Because he had

VRAAGT DE HEER VAN DE OOGST DAT HIJ WERKLIEDEN ZENDT IN ZIJN OOGST MT 9.38

Card distributed at Henri's ordination. "The harvest is rich but the laborers are few" (Mt 9:38).
(Nouwen family albums)

Left: Henri's ordination to the priesthood in July 1957.
(Nouwen family albums)

Henri, seated at left, with fellow seminarians. (Copyright: Louis ter Steeg, Utrecht)

distinguished himself at the seminary, he was offered the chance to go to Rome and continue his studies there. In this way he would be able to return to the Dutch church qualified to teach in the seminary or take some other leadership position in the church. Henri considered the proposal, and then he made a counterproposal: he did want to continue with his studies, but not in Rome. Instead of studying a theological topic in Rome, Henri proposed that he be permitted to seek a doctorate in psychology at Nijmegen University.

In 1957 psychology was a new and rather controversial field, most certainly for a Catholic priest. However, Cardinal Alfrink gave Henri his blessing to enter the university and begin these studies. It is a measure both of the cardinal's broadmindedness and of the optimistic and open-ended spirit of the times that Henri Nouwen was allowed to do this. Nijmegen was a Catholic university, and priests had studied there since its inception; however, the field of psychology was still new, influenced by challenging, even radical theories proposed by thinkers such as Sigmund Freud and Carl Jung. Their theories on human nature, on the unconscious, on sexuality, and on religion were radically at variance with the teachings of the Catholic Church. Yet Dutch Catholics were forging ahead, entering these new fields and establishing dialogue with everyone, even with the followers of such revolutionary thinkers.

Henri Nouwen remained close to his bishop, Bernard Alfrink, even after departing for the United States. The cardinal visited Henri Nouwen while Nouwen was at the Menninger Foundation in Kansas. The time came when some authority figures in the church, and the Vatican itself, became very unpopular in Holland, but Henri never felt that the ecclesiastical authorities merited this level of criticism. Much of his positive feelings for the hierarchy were because of his very good experience with his own bishop, Bernard Cardinal Alfrink, a true scholar and a true Christian.

"During the offertory I carefully held the chalice. After the consecration I lifted it high above my head. . . . The presence of Jesus was more real for me than the presence of any friend could possibly be. Afterwards, I knelt for a long time and was overwhelmed by the grace of my priesthood."
—Can You Drink the Cup?

(Nouwen family album)

Vatican II

Pope John XXIII, who convened the Second Vatican Council. (Courtesy Maryknoll archives)

The many initiatives that sprang up in Catholic circles in Europe after World War II did not lead to significant breakthroughs during the pontificate of Pius XII. In fact, most were suppressed. However, the pressure for change continued to build. The medieval mind-set of Catholicism needed updating, and the rigidity of nineteenth- and early-twentieth-century papal policies also cried out for review. Change finally came in the person of Pope John XXIII, a mild and open-hearted Italian who insisted that the windows be thrown open and the house of God aired out.

The watchword of his papacy was *aggiornamento,* Italian for "getting up to date," and the creation of the new models he had in mind would come about through the assembly of a general council of the church. In the biblical book of Acts the first Christians can be seen consulting each other and reaching consensus, and since the fourth century major issues and changes in the church have always been addressed by ecumenical councils, which are assemblies of all the bishops from every country.

The pope presides at any ecumenical council, but the work of preparation and direction of the councils is done by the Vatican, with input from bishops and theologians chosen for their reputation or expertise. In the case of the council called by Pope John, one of the bishops chosen to be an architect and director of the assembly's deliberations was Cardinal Alfrink, Henri Nouwen's bishop. This would be Alfrink's greatest contribution to Roman Catholicism. He was not only on the planning committee for the Council, he became an effective champion of progressive theology during the conciliar sessions. His effectiveness was augmented by several important factors: the Dutch church was united behind him, Holland had been experimenting with many of the changes proposed at the Council for a number of years, and he relied on expert theologians for advice, such as the Belgian, Edward Schillebeeckx, who had begun teaching at Nijmegen University the year that Henri Nouwen entered the student body.

In part because of Alfrink's and Schillebeeckx's leadership, the small nation of Holland had an inordinate influence over the assembly that came to be known as Vatican II. The Dutch church was able to provide a media and documentation center for the assembly in Rome. This media center served a vital function, providing position papers written by experts on all matters under discussion (handily translated into all major languages) and thus becoming an unofficial press room and informational clearinghouse for the many journalists who needed theological background information to interpret official press releases and who could not access many official Roman sources.

What became abundantly clear to all the participants in the conciliar process was that theology and ecclesial reform in Holland had advanced significantly. Many of the liturgical and procedural reforms suggested and eventually adopted at the council had been allowed experimentally in Holland for some time. These included the use of vernacular languages instead of Latin, the reception of communion in the hand, the use of laypeople as lectors and Eucharistic ministers, and many other hallmarks of the Vatican II liturgy.

Vatican II also made enormous strides in terms of ecumenism. There were Orthodox and Protestant observers invited to attend the council, and the council documents recognized the many contributions and integrity of other Christians, referred to for the first time as "separated brethren," not schismatics. In another important reversal, modernity itself was recognized by the council as a phenomenon requiring adaptation rather than condemnation.

Henri visiting the Vatican during the Council (Nouwen family albums)

"The churches of Rome are like beautiful frames around empty spaces witnessing to the One who is the quiet, still, center of all human life."
—Clowning in Rome

The world's bishops meeting at
Vatican II. (Courtesy Maryknoll archives)

"Often it seems harder
to believe in the Church
than to believe in God.
But whenever we separate
our belief in God from
our belief in the Church,
we become unbelievers.
God has given us the
Church as the place
where God becomes
God-with-us."

—Bread for the Journey

Monsignor Anton Ramselaar, Henri's uncle, was called to Rome to provide help and expertise concerning the role of the laity in the church and the issue of Catholic-Jewish relations, and he was able to take Henri Nouwen along and include him in his activities as an assistant. Henri was thus present in Rome during several council sessions and took a small part in the intense reconsideration of Catholic principles that took place there.

In fact, the philosophy of Vatican II was to play a defining role in Henri Nouwen's life and work. In later life Nouwen would lead his students and readers into a more humble, realistic, and Christ-centered spirituality. If we search for the origin and inspiration of his remarkable reformulation of the life of Christian faith, it becomes clear that he was drawing on the dramatic reformulation of Catholicism carried out by Schillebeeckx, Congar, Chenu, de Lubac, and the other theologians and bishops gathered in Rome that became known to the world as Vatican II. The council reinforced everything that Henri had absorbed in seminary and from the endless dialogues of the following years in Holland. Later, many of the principles of this great council came into question or were set aside, but Henri Nouwen continued to teach and to embody the high ideals of the council called by Pope John.

University Training

Even before Henri went with his uncle to attend the council, his world had opened up dramatically when he began his studies at Nijmegen. It is clear that entering the university was the beginning of an entirely new phase in the life of Henri Nouwen. He was to spend seven years actively engaged in the study of psychology at Nijmegen University. With his extroverted personality and sincere interest in people, he adapted well, even happily, to the endless discussions and debate that are a central part of university life.

At the university he stood out for his speaking ability and thorough involvement in the formal and informal discussions taking place everywhere. Nijmegen University, although a Catholic institution, attracted many students with questions about their faith or even anticlerical views, and Nouwen was often on the defensive. A new, more modern world was emerging, and this was the backdrop to university life in the late fifties and early sixties. Henri Nouwen came of age representing Catholicism in this shifting environment of new books, new ideas, and new forms of art and music. In this new era, being a priest living and working alongside other students was not easy, as we find illustrated in a reflection on the life of a campus minister he wrote a few years later:

[H]ow much questioning can a man take? Can he allow people to ask him all the time: Why are you a priest? Why do you believe in God? Why do you pray? Can he allow himself to be flexible all the time and willing to shift gears, to incorporate new ideas, to scrutinize new criticism and to question again his basic convictions? But this is

"Most of my past life has been built around the idea that my value depends on what I do. I made it through grade school, high school, and university. I earned my degrees and awards and I made my career. Yes, with many others, I fought my way up to the lonely top of a little success, a little popularity, a little power."
—The Path of Peace

Henri with fellow graduate students.
(Nouwen family albums)

exactly what happens, when students ask questions, because every question about the meaning of life is, at the same time, a question about the meaning of the ministry. The question, "Why do I live?" is at the same time the question, "Why are you a priest?" [5]

Within Henri's department, the challenges he faced were even greater. There was a strong philosophical and clinical cast to the Nijmegen psychology program. Models of normal and abnormal behavior, a myriad of tests and procedures, and statistical analysis were the basis of Nouwen's clinical training, but Henri was not always adept or interested in such technical subjects. He had an intuitive learning style, and, although passionately interested in human nature, did not have the scientific cast of mind necessary to be a real clinician.

On a more philosophical level, the subject of psychology in Europe at that time was still very much under the sway of the great thinkers who had refounded this discipline, Sigmund Freud and Carl Jung especially. They had a vast impact, not only on psychology, but on Western society in general, introducing such revolutionary concepts as the theory of the unconscious mind. Freud believed that the most basic aggressive and sexual instincts of life are driven from the conscious minds of modern people, and take up residence in the murky waters of the "unconscious." Because of repressing so much and the inevitable conflicts that arise in life, he thought everyone is pathological or neurotic to a greater or lesser extent. For the pessimistic Freud, religion was an illusion.

Carl Jung seemed to offer a more hopeful view of humanity and even of religion. He saw life and the human psyche in binary, yin-yang terms. If we are conscious, then we are also unconscious, and our unconscious is full of all those things that we suppress to become who we are. These buried elements do come to the surface later, however, often in ways that cause us distress. Jung embraced mythology and the anthropology of primitive peoples as sources of data for understanding the true

Henri with his parents, after passing qualifying exams in psychology.
(Nouwen family albums)

nature of the psyche. Religion he treated as another possible source, although as the son of a traumatized pastor, he felt ambivalent about Christianity.

As a priest studying psychology, Henri Nouwen must have had difficulties trying to reconcile his seminary training with the challenges of the new science of mind that he had chosen to study. Although a pioneer, he was not alone. Han Fortmann, also a priest, was on the psychology faculty and wrote on both spirituality and psychology. Although he was considered an authority in this area, Henri for some reason did not form a bond with Fr. Fortmann, nor was he much influenced by him, despite some expectations on the part of other priests of the diocese of Utrecht that this relationship would blossom. He obtained his doctorandus from Nijmegen, which is a professional qualification, but felt that any thesis he wrote would need to embrace theology and psychology in a way different from any approach taken by anyone in the Netherlands. Thus he began to look for models and for help beyond Holland and beyond Europe.

America Beckons

During the fifties and sixties the cultural and intellectual influence of the United States on Europe, especially on Great Britain, Holland, and Germany, grew steadily. The study of psychiatry and psychology in Holland was heavily influenced by trends in America. Through his reading of American works on psychology Henri became aware of a school of thought in the United States that combined psychology and religion. It was called the pastoral counseling movement. Henri was very intrigued with the idea of combining the insights of psychology with a religious perspective. He knew that if he were to write a thesis combining the two, then it would have to have a great deal of American input.

If he were to study this American initiative, he first needed more information. He also needed some good advice, and he thought he could best obtain both in the United States itself. Therefore he took an unpaid position as chaplain on the Holland-America cruise line, and thus assured that he would at least have passage to the United States. While on a cruise line stopover in Boston, Henri asked for an appointment to speak with Harvard psychologist Gordon Allport, one of the authors that he and his friends had been reading. Professor Allport was involved in the pastoral counseling movement and was able to give Henri some of the expert advice he needed. Allport told Henri that his best bet was to finish the doctoral thesis he was beginning to work on in Holland and then seek a fellowship at the Menninger Foundation in Kansas. The Foundation was becoming a center for those wishing to embrace a more multidisciplinary approach to psychology.

Henri accepted the advice he had received. It was clear from what Allport had told him that he should finish his degree in Holland. Thus Henri sat down to write a thesis and satisfy the final degree requirements. However, his choice of a topic was a strong indication of the direction in which he intended to take his career. He chose to write about American case study method in pastoral education.

Chaplain for the Holland-America line, entering New York harbor in 1962. (Nouwen family albums)

"I was deeply moved when, arriving by ship from Holland, I first saw the New York skyline."
—Sabbatical Journey

Anton Boisen

When Henri Nouwen began to write his doctoral thesis, there was one figure that caught and held his attention above all others: Anton Boisen. For Henri, finding Anton Boisen was a very important development, because if there is any one figure who provided Henri Nouwen early on with a model for his remarkable spiritual perspective, that person was Boisen. Henri read Boisen's books, visited with Boisen in America, and wrote extensively on Boisen for his doctoral degree. Among his papers, there is more material on Boisen than on any other figure. Why was Henri so fascinated with Anton Boisen?

Anton Boisen was a minister and a professional forester. He was born in Indiana in 1876. Like Henri's own family, the Boisen household was religiously and academically oriented. While still a young man beginning to make his way in the world, Boisen suffered a mental breakdown and was interned for a fifteen-month period in a mental ward. This illness and confinement was the turning point in Boisen's life. As he contemplated his precipitous descent into mental illness, he came to see the calamity as a call to repentance and self-examination. His life was laid bare, and Boisen found himself walking a spiritual and mental tightrope—paradoxically, he found himself both closer to God and closer to complete psychosis than at any time in his life.

How should he respond to this shattering experience? The medical interpretation of his illness he found to be cold, clinical, and lacking in meaning. The doctors seemed to understand illnesses and disease, but they did not understand Boisen himself. Anton Boisen believed that in the interpretation of his illness, there was much more hanging in the balance than reestablishing healthy mental functions. He thought that he as an individual was called to consider who he had become.

It was by means of such deep self-scrutiny that Anton Boisen fought his way back from depression and psychosis. Later, as he reflected on what he had been through, he realized that the people in his life, his own self-understanding, and even his religious and scientific training had all been instrumental in his regaining his mental health. His life had hung in the balance, and understanding his own life, in all its detailed singularity, had been the key to his recovery.

Today this may not seem like such a profound revelation, but in the early twentieth century Boisen's realization was a real departure from standard models of therapeutic care. When Boisen emerged from his illness and was released, he enrolled in Andover Newton seminary, and he also began taking classes at Harvard University. There he met Richard Cabot, a scion of a famous Boston family and a Harvard professor of medicine. Cabot was vitally interested in the case-study method. Together they explored the overlap between the insights they had developed independently; they agreed that individual cases required more than categorical, textbook responses. Cabot's own work led to the introduction of case-study methodology in medical studies at Harvard, and Boisen developed a theory of personal care that eschewed clinical categorization in favor of a review of the patient's life and philosophy. He saw the patient as a "living human text," one that must be carefully read and studied.

Anton Boisen was eventually appointed as chaplain in Worcester State Hospital, the principal state mental institution in Massachusetts. There he was able to promote a new collaborative relationship, really a therapeutic alliance, between clergy, medical personnel, and the patients. He began to visit seminaries and divinity schools to invite students to spend time in his hospital and in other medical settings. These efforts led to

"Making one's own wounds a source of healing, therefore, calls not for a sharing of superficial personal pains but for a constant willingness to see one's own pain and suffering as rising from the depth of the universal human condition."
—The Wounded Healer

Anton Boisen, the subject of Nouwen's dissertation. (Anton Boisen Estate. Courtesy Photograph Series, Henri Nouwen Archives)

"In a way we can say that Boisen's own psychosis became the center of his identity. He became the 'man who went through the wilderness of the lost' and he made his own illness the focus of his life. There he found his true vocation: the ministry to the mentally ill."

—Pastoral Psychology
(September 1968)

the establishment of what is now called clinical pastoral education, a standard component in most seminary programs.

Boisen wrote a series of books, spoke widely, and gained a following. However, he was a tragic figure. His mental health was never 100 percent assured. He was a passionate, troubled individual who made a great impact on the world, not despite his problems, but because of his troubled perspective. He was a wounded healer whose own woundedness was a personal source of divine knowledge. From Anton Boisen Henri Nouwen drew direct inspiration for his own ministry. He learned from Boisen that one's own psychological troubles and weakness could be a source of inspiration and a path to God, something that would become a hallmark of his spiritual writing and speaking. Henri once wrote, quoting Boisen:

"To be plunged as a patient into a hospital for the insane may be tragedy or it may be an opportunity. For me it has been an opportunity." No better words can express the importance of Boisen's illness, as these opening lines of his main work. Boisen's hospitalization not only was an opportunity for him, but even the focal experience of his life. So far as he was concerned, without it, "there would have been no new light upon the interrelatedness of mental disorder and religious experience. Neither would there have been any clinical training movement." We cannot stress enough the centrality of this experience to Boisen's life and the great ideas and events which came out of it. Everything he did and said since that moment was "in the light of my own experience." [6]

> *"As Jesus ministers, so he wants us to minister. He wants Peter to feed his sheep and care for them, not as 'professionals' who know their clients' problems and take care of them, but as vulnerable brothers and sisters who know and are known, who care and are cared for, who forgive and are being forgiven, who love and are being loved."*
> —In the Name of Jesus

The Menninger Foundation

(Nouwen family albums)

Henri Nouwen presented a prospectus for the thesis he wanted to write about American case-study methods—Boisen and Cabot's big topic—to the faculty of the psychology department at Nijmegen University, but it was not accepted. Henri was told that his thesis plan would need to be revised and recast in the form of a more clinical study based on quantitative data and analysis. Henri balked at this attempt to "straightjacket" him and withdrew his prospectus. He left Nijmegen with his doctorandus, a professional qualification, rather than a doctoral research degree.

Nouwen's next stop was Kansas, U.S.A. He had been successful in obtaining a fellowship in religion and psychiatry at the Menninger Foundation, as Gordon Allport suggested he do. Karl Menninger was a famous figure in American medical circles and American society in general, and his books, such as *Man against Himself* and *Love against Hate,* were widely read and discussed. He had started the Menninger Foundation in 1925, along with his father and brother, who were also psychiatrists. The Menningers had a vision for "a better kind of medicine and a better kind of world." In 1946 they founded a school of psychiatry that quickly became the largest training center in the country, not only for psychiatrists, but for psychologists and other mental health professionals, too. At their foundation the Menningers pioneered a new therapy they called the "bio-psycho-social approach," a therapy that attended to the overall needs of the patient, an approach very much akin to Anton Boisen's concept of attending to the whole person. In fact, they implemented clinical pastoral education, Boisen's own brainchild, in their program for religion and psychiatry.

In these years there were numerous veterans of World War II who were in need of psychological and psychiatric attention, and the Menninger Foundation was one of the principal institutions providing treatment for them. Although they worked in a hospital setting, they tried to introduce some aspects of psychoanalysis to hospital treatment and to involve every aspect of life on a hospital ward in the recovery process. This became known as "milieu therapy."

At the Menninger Foundation in 1964, the year Henri Nouwen arrived, he would have been able to experience first-hand the kind of integrative, psycho-pastoral approach that he had dreamed of doing in Holland. Many of the most influential figures doing work of this sort in the United States had connections with the Foundation. In fact, Henri was quite fortunate in his timing, because the Menninger Foundation was never more open to the integration of religion and medicine than it was in the time when Henri Nouwen was in residence. Seward Hiltner, a Princeton professor who had also encouraged Henri to go to Menninger, looks back on that period as the "golden age of religion and psychiatry at the Foundation."[7]

"Religion" at the Foundation meant Protestantism, Judaism, and Catholicism, pretty much in that order. Henri was thus confronted anew with the new ecumenical reality that he had encountered more and more often in Holland. Some of those who had arrived in Kansas to work in this mixed milieu had difficulty integrating religion and the sciences of the mind, but Henri embraced with gusto the ecumenism and the interdisciplinary approach. He completed some clinical assessments, especially one on a troubled adolescent, practiced and improved his English, and took part in the training offered to the interns and psychologists working around him. The figure of Karl Menninger impressed him greatly. One story that eventually found its way into one of his books concerned Menninger as teacher:

(Nouwen family albums)

"Medicine, psychiatry, and social work all offer us models in which 'service' takes place in a one-way direction. Someone serves, someone else is being served, and be sure not to mix up the roles! . . . The world in which we live . . . has no models to offer to those who want to be shepherds in the way Jesus was a shepherd."

—In the Name of Jesus

Nouwen with Cardinal Alfrink (right), during the latter's visit to the Menninger Foundation in 1965.
(Nouwen family albums)

One day Dr. Karl Menninger, the well-known psychiatrist, asked a class of psychiatric residents what the most important part of the treatment process of mental patients was. Some said the psychotherapeutic relationship to the doctor. Some said giving recommendations for future behavior. Others said the prescription of drugs. Others said the continuing contact with the family after the treatment in the hospital had ended. And there were still different viewpoints. But Karl Menninger did not accept any of these answers as the right one. His answer was "diagnosis." The first and most important task of the healer is making the right diagnosis. Without an accurate diagnosis, subsequent treatment has little effect. [8]

Menninger had a far-reaching vision that transcended mere clinical insight. Henri was at an impressionable age, and he eagerly embraced Menninger's expanded vision of medicine, health, and a better world. He took part in many meetings and groups, including one for Catholics working at the Menninger Foundation. Henri was the youngest and least experienced member of this group, but it furnished him with important models for integrating some of the Menninger insights, and psychology generally, with Catholicism. There he met John Dos Santos, and after Dos Santos was called to Notre Dame to create a department of psychology there, he remembered the young Dutch priest and wrote to Nouwen at the Foundation, asking him to be part of that effort.

Notre Dame

Thus it was that Henri Nouwen got a job at Notre Dame, the first institution in the United States to see him not as a student, but as a professor, not as a learner, but as a teacher. The year was 1966. John Dos Santos, the Notre Dame chairperson, had expected that Henri would join in the teaching and research activities in the new psychology department, and that he would help him win over some of the Notre Dame senior faculty with regard to this new discipline, because Henri Nouwen, like them, was a priest. However, the research focus of the psychology department was highly scientific. Henri listened to an account of some of the department's projects concerning perception and cognition and told Dos Santos and the rest of the department that he had little interest in pursuing this type of scientific research. Finding himself in such a formally scientific department helped him to realize anew that his primary vocation was to theology rather than clinical psychology.

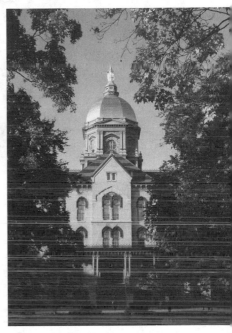

University of Notre Dame. (Courtesy Notre Dame)

Nevertheless he did teach a class in personality development for the psychology department, Nouwen's first, and as a result, there sprang up a devoted group of Nouwen friends and followers among the students. As he became better known at Notre Dame and made new contacts, his connections with the psychology department diminished. Before long he had become an adjunct to the pastoral theology department and he dropped his ties to the psychology department completely.

Henri was discovering more about America also. These were the years of the civil rights movement, and Henri took part in demonstrations and activities supportive of the black

Nouwen took this picture during the 1965 civil rights march in Selma, Alabama. (Courtesy Photograph Series, Henri Nouwen Archives)

"I will never forget the joy I experienced during that march. . . .They all looked to me like saints, radiant with God's love."
—Our Greatest Gift

community's struggle to emerge from their status as second-class citizens. Henri made an automatic and unambivalent identification with the message of Martin Luther King and the yearning of black Americans for equality. He not only participated in rallies and traveled to demonstrations, he also wrote on the subject of civil rights for publication back on Holland.

There was good chemistry in Henri's connection to the United States. He liked the country, and the country liked him. At Notre Dame he began developing his own style of writing and speaking and became something of a campus character. In Holland he was remembered by other graduate students as a serious person, always deep in thought and preoccupied by difficult questions, but in America this began to change. Perhaps the personal fulfillment of working at the Menninger Foundation and Notre Dame caused him to loosen up, and maybe the less formal American style rubbed off on him.

Henri was also finding that the questions that most interested him—spiritual or philosophical questions about intimacy, personal confusion, and identity—were interesting to others, too. One of the students following his lectures was a journalist from the *National Catholic Reporter,* and this student asked permission to publish one of his lectures in that journal. Response to that publication was so positive that further essays were published, and then gathered into Nouwen's first book: *Intimacy: Essays in Pastoral Psychology.*

The sixties were a special time for Catholics all around the world. There was a sense that change was in the air. Vatican II had drawn to a close in 1965, the year before Henri arrived at Notre Dame. Catholics at Notre Dame and elsewhere were grasping for explanations of the proposed changes, and they were seeking new models. Henri Nouwen, as a Dutch priest, found that he had a head start in facing and understanding the new Catholicism. He had been living the Vatican II lifestyle in Holland for much of the last decade, and he had been present in Rome during the council sessions. He thus became a conduit of Vatican II thinking and spirituality for Notre Dame and the American Midwest. As he did so, he also began taking on a persona that would later become his trademark—intense, zany, and humble all at once. Here is a description of Henri preparing to say mass in August 1966, given by his friend, Fr. Don McNeill:

Notre Dame library. (Courtesy Notre Dame)

> *His hair was all over the place and he was running around making sure the cruets for the wine and the bread were taken care of before the Mass began. I didn't know who he was. I even wondered if he was someone who was able to celebrate the Eucharist. But when he began to speak there was an immediate magnetism—all of us were awestruck by his passion and insights. As he continued the Mass, his reverence and emanation of light released us from our stereotypical expectations of priesthood.* [9]

"I never planned to be a writer and I have never really thought of myself as a writer. In fact, my father always used to say that I didn't have more than three hundred words in my vocabulary."
—The Critic, Summer 1978

So it was that Henri Nouwen became an agent of change and of renewal in America. He had begun to expound his penetrating insights into the spiritual life of modern people, and

"I have always used as my prime resource some of my own observations and my own personal struggles with whatever I am writing about."
—The Critic, Summer 1978

(Copyright: M.R. Kronstien. Courtesy Photograph Series, Henri Nouwen Archives)

with his crazy, intense personal style, he surprised and then quickly won over his new, American audience. Being an exemplar of change and renewal would be his principal role in the United States and then in other parts of the Western world for the rest of his life. Notre Dame opened up this new and very important stage in his journey.

Problems in Holland

When the two one-year contracts that he had made with Notre Dame expired, it was time for Nouwen to return to Holland. He had decided to renew his bid for a doctorate. He ended up living in Utrecht and joining the faculty of the Catholic Theological Institute there, where he taught classes and supervised students. He also worked at the Pastoral Institute in Amsterdam. His plan was to rework his earlier thesis idea, focusing more on Anton Boisen as a study in acute psychosis and conversion, and present this to the theology department of Nijmegen University as a thesis in pastoral theology. Of course, to obtain a doctorate in theology there were other requirements—examinations in a range of topics, including pastoral theology, psychology, sociology, and catechetics—all of which he set about fulfilling.

Nouwen was back in the land of his birth, and his work was surely moving forward. However, this was a difficult time in his life. He felt rather lonely and out of step with the Catholic community in Holland. Having made such a public and international contribution to progressive theology during the years of the Vatican Council, the Dutch had moved ahead enthusiastically with other proposals and new experiments. However, conservative elements in the Vatican were determined to check the Dutch church's apparent drift in a more liberal direction.

The Vatican curia responded to the changes taking place in Holland with an effort to promote to the episcopacy only those Dutch priests who took a position opposing the many new initiatives of the Dutch church. The result of these reac-

"It is hard to explain why Holland changed from a very pious to a very secular country in one generation. Many reasons can be given. But it seems to me, from just looking around and meeting and speaking to people, that this captivating prosperity is one of the more obvious reasons. . . . The Dutch have become a distracted people—very good, kind, and good-natured, but caught in too much of everything."
—Road to Daybreak

"I often wonder where I would be today if I had been part of the great turmoil of the Dutch Church during the last decades. Blaming is not the issue. What is important is to find the anger-free parts in people's hearts where God's love can be heard and received."

—The Road to Daybreak

tionary appointments to the episcopacy was to alarm and alienate the many Dutch believers who had worked so hard for change. The Dutch church quickly became angry and polarized. Those priests who were most popular with the people were the ones who spoke out against the repressive stance of the hierarchy and the Vatican. Many of these same priests ultimately left the priesthood, and the churches themselves began to empty out as well. As part of this polarization those who had been reformers were often transformed into militants with whom Henri could not identify. In fact, Henri had criticized the militant liberalism of the Dutch church as part of an example he gave in his first book:

A young deacon in Holland paid a house visit to a middle-aged couple and explained to them in convincing terms that birth control was no longer a problem, that they had no reason to be concerned about their son who had stopped going to church, that celibacy would go out the window within a decade and that most devotions were perfect examples of magic. After his exposition the mother of the house thought for a while and then said meditatively: "Nothing has really changed." "How do you mean?" asked the deacon. "Well," she mused, "twenty years ago the priests told us what we should do and believe. Now, with the same intolerance, they tell us what we should not do and not believe. After all the problem is still the same." [10]

Henri Nouwen's reaction to the polarized and disintegrating state of Dutch Catholicism that met him when he returned home was one of dismay and despair. Not only did he disagree with the direction in which most Catholics seemed to be moving, he found that he was the odd man out. A consensus had been reached in the years that he had been in America, and he was not part of it. Now, he seemed to lack the vocabulary and the standing to even address the very real problems the Catholic community was facing. Then, to make matters worse, his doctoral dissertation topic in theology was also rejected, on the grounds that it lacked both a statistical base and theological depth. Faced with the prospect of starting over, he abandoned this second attempt to secure a doctoral degree in Nijmegen and accepted a second doctorandus.

It was truly a bleak time. Even though Henri Nouwen had arrived home, no one seemed to realize that he was there nor did anyone extend to him the sort of invitations to speak or teach or publish that he expected would come his way. At one point he withdrew from the teaching of seminarians and lived alone in a rented room. He was becoming, in his own words, "morose, angry, sour, hateful, bitter and complaining."[11] Although he knew he needed the solitude to write, the sense of rejection and alienation that were part of this period were truly terrible. He had worked hard and traveled far, and the result apparently was loneliness and frustration.

Nouwen by the canal in Utrecht, 1970. (Nouwen family albums)

Interestingly enough, it was at this dark point that Nouwen began to do some of his first significant writing. He published *Creative Ministry,* his reflections on how to live a ministry that was truly spiritual, submitting to an American publisher an English-language manuscript he had largely completed at Notre Dame. He also began work on two more manuscripts in Dutch, one of which would ultimately become one of his most famous books, *The Wounded Healer.*

This was surely a paradoxical moment and a turning point in his life: He was faced with rejection, and found he could conform neither to the common opinions of Dutch Catholics nor to the scientific and intellectual rigor required by the University of Nijmegen. He wrote in isolation, yet nevertheless began to produce the books of theological and spiritual reflection that would ultimately become his greatest gift to the church and the world. He was not well received in Holland, but this new style of writing was resonating with publishers and readers in America, a land that had apparently not forgotten him.

Professor at Yale Divinity School. (Courtesy Yale Divinity School)

Yale

Henri Nouwen's first book, *Intimacy,* had interested and impressed the dean and several faculty members at Yale Divinity School. For that reason Henri had been invited to speak at Yale while he was teaching at Notre Dame, and while he was in Holland he received another request that he lecture at Yale. On that visit from Holland to Connecticut he was given a surprise interview and even a job offer. However, Henri declined. He had decided that his future was at home, in the Netherlands.

However, interest in Nouwen at Yale did not diminish. As he continued to produce a number of engaging and practical books and articles in English, the divinity school renewed its offer. Nouwen hesitated. The offer from Yale was attractive, but he wanted time to finish projects in Holland, and he insisted that if he went to Yale, he could not be expected to produce technical works of scholarship like the rest of the faculty. This had been his downfall several times already.

Yale agreed to Nouwen's terms and he decided to join the divinity school faculty. He was to be the psychological half of a two-person team working in the field of pastoral ministry. However, in the end this arrangement or division of labor never came to pass. Much as had happened when he was recruited to join the psychology department at Notre Dame, once Henri arrived at Yale, he found his interest in representing the psychological approach to be waning further and being replaced by a strong desire to weave personal spirituality back into pastoral ministry. Indeed, by this point spirituality had become his primary focus.

"I experienced it in my own seminary years and saw it at Notre Dame, at the North American College, at Yale Divinity School, and at many other places. Everywhere there was the tendency to live, act, and think as if the real life is not here but there, not now but later. This tendency makes the formation of community so difficult, if not impossible."

—¡Gracias!

Although Yale got something different than they had bargained for, Nouwen's contribution to the life of the school was huge and innovative. During his time at Yale Nouwen taught classes on ministry to prisoners and to the elderly, on ministry in secular institutions, on discipleship, on the relationship of ministry and spirituality, on the ministry of Vincent van Gogh, on prayer, and on Thomas Merton. Besides his academic courses, Nouwen became a de facto chaplain to the Yale student body and community. Henri Nouwen was one of the first Roman Catholics to join the Protestant faculty of this storied and famous American academic institution. His celebration of mass in the basement chapel of the school became a staple of community life at Yale, and these services were attended by students from a wide variety of backgrounds.

His popularity as a professor was matched by a growing reputation as a spiritual writer. In the ten years he was to remain at Yale he was more and more widely read and quoted as an authority in the field of pastoral ministry and spirituality. In addition, Henri Nouwen ended up spending more time with students than any other faculty member, and he made friendships with dozens of them that would last for decades. As students began to arrive at Yale specifically because of Nouwen's presence there, some of the faculty did become somewhat envious. This was understandable. Henri Nouwen was completely different from them in a number of ways. As a Catholic he provided a splash of color in an otherwise very traditional atmosphere, and while they toiled in the library to produce serious works of scholarship, he dashed off little books on spiritual themes that anyone might read and enjoy. They were serious scholars, but he was the popular one who everyone was reading.

Although there was faculty resentment of Nouwen's fame and his popularity among the students, Yale was a very good place for Henri Nouwen to expand and deepen his mission to America and the world. It was at Yale that Nouwen rounded

Teaching with his whole body.
(Photo by Ron van den Bosch, used with permission)

out his persona as a humble seeker with a magical insight into matters of the human heart. It was at Yale that he learned to speak more openly about his own spiritual journey instead of using textbook examples and other abstractions, and it was at Yale that he found the forum to speak about the civil rights movement, American foreign policy, and the many other concerns that were shaking the nation and the world.

Nouwen was granted tenure at Yale in 1974, some three years after his arrival. For most people, achieving tenure at an Ivy League school is the highest rung on the professional ladder and represents the culmination of a long career. For Nouwen, Yale was a good place to be, but not one where he expected to stay forever. There was a restlessness in Nouwen that had been part of his temperament since he was a small child, and that same restlessness asserted itself more and more

This chapel at Yale Divinity School has since been named the Henri Nouwen Chapel. (Courtesy Yale Divinity School)

"When I asked to come to Yale, my bishop said I could go for a few years; I stayed ten. Meanwhile, I became an associate professor, then a tenured, full professor. I was doing well on the level of my ambitions. . . . But I began to question whether I was really doing God's will."

—The Road to Peace

in the decade he remained at Yale. In spite of his success in ministering to students, teaching ministry, and writing interesting books for the wider public, he was feeling increasingly hollow and ungrounded. If he were to apply his theory about personal spirituality at the heart of ministry to his own person, he knew that the conclusion would be that his own spirit was broken and his sense of certainty very tenuous. He knew he ought to be closer to God than he was, ought to be doing more than he was, and so he was forever searching the horizon for some new person or interest or activity to give him a greater sense of fulfillment.

Merton

Besides Anton Boisen, Henri Nouwen was most deeply influenced by one other writer, also American, named Thomas Merton. Merton had originally been a university intellectual and hipster. Part of the previous generation, he would have been seventeen years older than Henri himself. When he was a young man Merton converted to Catholicism and embarked on a search for a deeper vocation; his journey took him through various changes in lifestyle, as he moved from critic to inquirer, then to teacher in a Catholic college, and ultimately to the enclosed life of a Cistercian monk. The Cistercian community was one of the strictest of monastic orders, living in real seclusion and even using sign language to avoid unnecessary speaking.

Thomas Merton. (Photo by Jim Forest, used with permission)

Although Merton submitted to the formation and discipline of the Cistercians, or Trappists, as they are sometimes called, he was not destined to be an ordinary monk. A brilliant innovator and gifted writer, he composed an account of his journey to the doors of the monastery that became a spiritual classic. This book was called *The Seven Storey Mountain.* Through this memoir and a number of provocative publications on the spiritual life, he suddenly became quite famous, and that renown and influence continue to the present day. Merton's unique vision proved to be a transformative element that has enlivened and shaped all subsequent attempts to live the monastic life in the Western church. It has also had a dramatic impact on Christian thinking generally. From within his monastic enclosure Thomas Merton engaged problems of war and peace, the civil rights movement, Latin American injustice,

(Photo by Robert Lax, used with permission)

"As his life grew in spiritual maturity, Merton came to see with a penetrating clarity that solitude did not separate him from his contemporaries but instead brought him into a deep communion with them. . . . The more he was able to convert his restless loneliness into a solitude of heart, the more he could discover the pains of his world in his own inner center and respond to them."

—Reaching Out

various spiritual authors of previous centuries, and Zen Buddhism. He published journals, such as *The Sign of Jonas,* that ranked as spiritual classics, and books on prayer, spiritual direction, and personal ethics.

Henri Nouwen had met and talked with Merton on a visit to his Kentucky monastery and he regarded Merton as an extremely valuable guide regarding the question of how to address modern society from a spiritual perspective. But that was only one thing that Nouwen was learning from him. Merton's writings were revolutionizing Catholic monasticism and Christian spirituality by communicating an up-to-date and realistic sense of what faith actually felt like; furthermore, Merton's inclusion of all sorts of elements from outside Catholicism was brilliant. He was the ultimate exemplar of what Henri Nouwen might want to be. Merton was interpreting the tradition anew from a very cultured and informed perspective, but one that nevertheless remained Catholic and embraced the living monasticism of the church. Nouwen was not his only admirer; even Pope John XXIII sent to Merton the stole he had worn while being installed as pope, an unmistakable sign of approval.

Merton was to solidify for Nouwen the conviction that a life of prayer should ideally center around a kind of contemplation that took the world in, understood it, and saw in it the coming of Jesus. Merton was a writer and an artist, and thus there was an unmistakable artistic element in his teachings on prayer and the spiritual life. Merton dared to be creative, and saw prayer as a kind of seeing and of expression. In ways small and large Nouwen absorbed the teachings of Merton and made them his own. Thomas Merton was a guide and a model of someone who had made a dramatic impact on many others through writings that were faithfully Christian but also creative and even daring.

Although Merton was a much deeper thinker than Henri Nouwen, Thomas Merton exemplified for Nouwen the kind of awakened and inspired Christian writer who was fully engaged with his faith and reaching out to learn from and interact with the world. Nouwen had begun to think seriously about Merton after he returned to Holland. There he wrote a book about Merton that he later translated into English and published as *Pray to Live*. He taught a class at Yale on Merton and then revised his book on Merton, calling it this time *Thomas Merton: Contemplative Critic*. In the Yale years Merton continued to be a pivotal model for Nouwen. Psychology as a framework was receding for Henri, and in its place were creativity, contemplation, and engagement in the spiritual life.

Abbey of Gethsemani. (Courtesy Abbey of Gethsemani)

"Thomas Merton invites us to an always deeper awareness of the incomprehensibility of God. He continually unmasks the illusions that we know God and so frees us to see the Lord in always new and surprising ways."
—The Road to Peace

Monasticism

Abbot John Eudes Bamberger of the Abbey of the Genesee. (Photo by Brother Anthony Weber)

Opposite:
Nouwen praying in the chapel choir at Genesee. (Photo by Brother Anthony Weber)

It was certainly Thomas Merton who first drew Henri Nouwen to Gethsemani, the Trappist monastery in Kentucky where Merton lived, but once acquainted with the prayerful lifestyle of the monks, and after he had made some friends and contacts there, his interest in monasticism itself and the Cistercians greatly increased. On a visit he made in 1964 he told the monastery guest master that he would soon be going to Notre Dame to help found a department of psychology there. This led to him being introduced to John Eudes Bamberger, one of Thomas Merton's disciples. Besides being a monk, Bamberger was a medical doctor and had undertaken formal training in Freudian psychoanalysis. Nouwen found himself bonding immediately with Fr. John Eudes and pursued him with questions about psychology, spirituality, and his own life. This relationship with Fr. John Eudes evolved into one of spiritual direction and grew over the years. When Nouwen's *Intimacy* appeared in 1969, it was dedicated to John Eudes Bamberger.

As time passed Nouwen began to grow truly enamored of what Merton and Bamberger represented—prayer centered around an immersion in the liturgy, individual growth as part of a community, and oversight by an abbot or another monk who had made progress in the life of the Spirit. Nouwen began to wonder if he himself did not belong in a monastery. Thomas Merton was proof that becoming a monk need not spell the end of inquiry, books, ideas, and even writing. Indeed, monasticism seemed to provide the structure and the companionship that made Christianity make most sense.

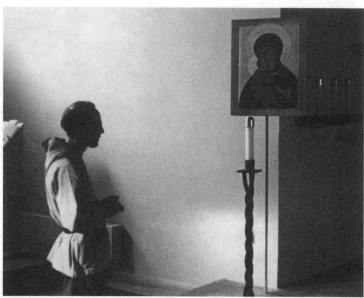

(Photo by Brother Anthony Weber)

Fr. John Eudes was providing Henri with spiritual direction, and when John Eudes went to Piffard, New York, to establish and direct a new monastery there, this move brought him much closer to Nouwen at Yale. As contacts between the two men continued, Nouwen thought perhaps he might obtain permission to spend a longer period at the monastery, despite the normal prohibitions against extended visits. He asked Fr. John Eudes about this possibility; the abbot consulted the community, and it was agreed that Henri could go to the Genesee, as the monastery in New York was called, for a longer stay. The year was 1974, and Henri Nouwen had just been granted tenure at Yale. Once in the monastic establishment at Piffard, Henri shaved his head, put on the garb of a novice, and joined the community in all its work activities and life of prayer. He also delighted in the opportunity to consult Fr. John Eudes more frequently.

What Nouwen found in that seven-month stay among the Trappists was that the physical labor involved in baking bread, sawing wood, hauling rocks, and all the other very physical tasks set before him were almost more than he could handle. Nor was the isolation and solitude of the monastery as beneficial and quieting as he had hoped. On the contrary, he found that all of his uncertainties and personal faults were more apparent and more troublesome than ever.

Normally accustomed to a wide range of stimulating human contacts, he found himself feeling increasingly upset, lonely, and restless. He wrote letter after letter and then waited anxiously for replies. Through this challenging experience of living within Cistercian monasticism John Eudes tried to help him become more centered in himself and more tranquil through a combination of meditation and the use of the Jesus Prayer, which is the repetition of a short phrase accompanied by a disciplined avoidance of thoughts and distractions. Henri made a good attempt to calm himself, but he became more conscious of his inability to live the Cistercian lifestyle.

Nevertheless, the sense that Henri had that in John Eudes he was meeting with an authentic representative of a contemplative tradition and a gifted abbot remained strong. John Eudes was deeply involved in the study of the desert fathers, the first Christian hermits to enter the Egyptian desert and engage in a spirited mental and physical campaign to transform themselves and find God. Thomas Merton had been the first to realize the importance of the desert fathers as a model for contemporary monastics, and John Eudes was furthering Merton's work by investigating the writings of Evagrius Ponticus, one of the great thinkers and writers who lived in the desert.

In fact, in 1981 John Eudes would publish the first book on Evagrius ever written in English. The abbot shared some of these studies and his insights with Henri Nouwen, and this added a new dimension to Henri's understanding of monasticism. He came to feel that among the monks, particularly this order that had been home to Thomas Merton, he was in touch with a tradition that embraced all of life and had produced true spiritual masters. Despite the great difficulties Nouwen exper-

"Dear Lord, this afternoon I shared my feelings of guilt and sinfulness with one of the monks. He gave me good advice. He kept urging me to move away continually from introspection and self-preoccupation and to concentrate on expressing my love for you."
—A Cry for Mercy

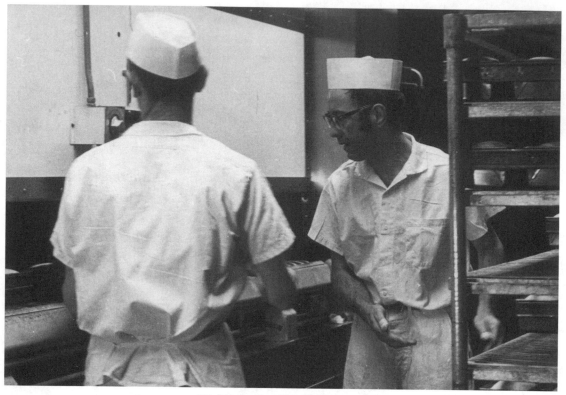

Working in the abbey bakery. (Photo by Brother Anthony Weber)

"At 4:15 A.M. I started working on the hot-bread line. The wheat bread came out of the oven so fast I couldn't get it on the racks and into the cooling room fast enough. Happily, John Baptist helped me out and prevented the bread from flying around. Meanwhile, I burned my arm on a hot pan. Stupid."

—Genesee Diary

enced while living the monastic lifestyle, he was forever changed by that first long stay at the monastery. There would be many other visits and one more extended stay in 1979. Although he realized that he was not cut out for monastic isolation, the ideals and the vision of monastic spirituality informed all that he did from then on.

Two Groundbreaking Books

The example of Thomas Merton was inspirational for Nouwen during his monastic stay, especially Merton's example of writing and praying from a place of solitude. By this point in his life Nouwen saw his ministry more and more in terms of being a writer on topics concerning spirituality, but he had not yet begun to write the kind of transparent books full of vivid feeling, honesty, and self-examination for which he would ultimately be best known. Instead, Nouwen in his early years was usually seen as an insightful and creative new voice on the pastoral theology scene.

It was while Henri Nouwen was living the monastic life and in spiritual direction with John Eudes that he produced the first book to reveal more fully the difficulties he wrestled with and the questions that nagged him while pursuing a deeper spiritual life. What Nouwen did was to publish the journal he kept while living in the monastery. *The Genesee Diary* marked a real departure for Nouwen, because in it he revealed like never before the daily irritations, doubts, and troubles that clouded his heart and with which he battled in the solitude of the monastic setting. This was risky. Writing in this way might have alienated many potential readers—Nouwen might have come off as too personal or even a bit scandalous—but the result of his publishing *The Genesee Diary* was that Henri Nouwen's popularity as a writer greatly increased.

Just as his first publications on intimacy while at Notre Dame had surprised many with their authenticity, publication of *The Genesee Diary* made many people realize that even a priest and an authority on spirituality could have doubts and fears just like

(Photo by Brother Anthony Weber)

"One of the things a monastery like this does for you is give you a new rhythm, a sacred rhythm."
—The Genesee Diary

them. Nouwen had opened his heart to his readers and received a positive response, and from that point forward he became a more personal, confessional writer, in the spirit of St. Augustine.

Another book that took shape during his stay at the Genesee was *Reaching Out: The Three Movements of the Spiritual Life.* He had taught the material contained in this book at Yale, but his stay at the monastery gave him time to edit and refine the manuscript for publication. *Reaching Out* sets out for the first time a basic description of the spiritual life on Nouwen's terms. As Henri explained, there are three fundamental areas, or relationships, that are key to an authentic spirituality: a relationship to one's self, a relationship to others, and a relationship to God. This threefold framework was something that would become part of his normal approach in later writings.

Indeed, when one reads *Reaching Out* one finds a surprisingly complete and mature expression of Nouwen's spirituality. Henri Nouwen would refine and improve his writing as he grew older, but his message would not change. *Reaching Out* and *The Genesee Diary* set the tone. He was by this point able to speak openly about his own sense of confusion, his restlessness, his yearning for God, and even his anger. He spoke to his readers as a preacher or spiritual director might, describing spiritual problems and mentioning examples, and then giving thoughtful solutions. He had abandoned his earlier identification with professional psychology, but his writing has an unmistakable psychological cast, as can be seen in his decision to focus spiritual attention in *Reaching Out* on the self and on others, not merely on God. Finally, he was learning to speak to "the average informed reader," using vocabulary and arguments that were in no way technical, but appealed to experience and to observations made by interesting authors such as Thoreau, the mystics of the church, the Zen masters, Kahlil Gibran, or Tolstoy. Like a preacher, sometimes he used examples that were drawn from the newspaper or from people with whom he had recently spoken. Henri Nouwen had found his voice.

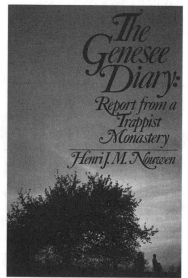

Cover of The Genesee Diary, *published in 1976.*

"A monastery is not built to solve problems but to praise the Lord in the midst of them."

—The Genesee Diary

Working in the abbey library.
(Photo by Brother Anthony Weber)

One passage from *Reaching Out* seems most representative of this period. In it, he deals with some of the same issues he had been describing in *The Genesee Diary*. Although he offers here what seems to be general advice, all of the problems he describes are ones that were troubling him in a very personal way while living in the monastery:

Living together with friends is an exceptional joy, but our lives will be sad if that becomes the aim of our strivings. Having a harmonious team working in unity of heart and mind is a gift from heaven, but if our own sense of worth depends on that situation we are sad people. Letters of friends are good to receive, but we should be able to live happily without them. Visits are gifts to be valued, but without them we should not fall into the temptation of a brooding mood. Phone calls, "just to say hello," can fill us with gratitude, but when we expect them as a necessary way to sedate our fear of being left alone, we are becoming the easy victims of our self-complaints. We are always in search of a community that can offer us a sense of belonging, but it is important to realize that being together in one house, one city or one country is only secondary to the fulfillment of our legitimate desire. Friendship and community are, first of all, inner qualities allowing human togetherness to be the playful expression of a much larger reality. They can never be claimed, planned or organized, but in our innermost self the place can be formed where they can be received as gifts. [12]

(Photo by David Schaefer. Courtesy Photograph Series, Henri Nouwen Archives)

The Teacher

Through what was becoming a string of popular books Henri Nouwen was by this point making a big impression on Christian circles in the United States. Whenever surveys were taken of ministers asking who they were reading and who they admired, Nouwen was at or near the top of the list. A number of universities around the country had invited him to be their commencement speaker and had awarded him honorary doctorates. He previewed his books in all the major Catholic magazines, and his books themselves were on the shelves of nearly every Christian bookstore. The same could not be said for many other authors, because Nouwen was one of the few who appealed to both Protestants and Catholics.

Despite huge success as a writer of spiritual books, it must be said that writing was not the realm where Henri was most effective. As good a writer as he was, he was even more persuasive as a speaker and teacher. There are two important aspects to his great speaking ability, and we will consider each in turn.

First of all, Henri was a remarkable, even gifted teacher in any one-to-one personal encounter. When he talked to someone, he was unassuming, and showed no sign that he felt superior or different from the person he was talking to, nor did he launch into long explanations or deal in abstractions. Instead, he focused so intently on the person with whom he was speaking that he seemed to forget everything else. Indeed, Henri really cared about others and made such deep friendships with people everywhere that it hardly seems possible for one person to have had so many friends. He spent hours on the phone

"To be a teacher is to disclose through your own person this mystery of God. The recognition of this mystery does not solve our problems or answer our questions, but it leads us closer to the source of all life and all love."
—Union Seminary Quarterly Review *(Fall 1976)*

(Courtesy Henri Nouwen Literary Centre)

"I think that real teaching and preaching should create community, create a joyful recognition of being a part of the same human condition."

—The Critic, Summer 1978

talking to people all over the world, would send books to everyone who wrote to him, engaged in correspondence with many of them, and ministered in this way to thousands of people, one by one.

In addition, Henri had a style of public preaching and teaching that was very moving. In fact, he could be ranked as one of the great twentieth-century communicators of the gospel. Self-effacing and personal, he was also animated and inspired as a speaker. He would literally jump around the stage and wave his arms, as if carried forward by the force of the vision within him. What with his curious accent, his thin frame of a body being tugged this way and that by the power of his inspiration, plus his utter sincerity and intensity, he held his audiences spellbound. This was a simple but clearly an inspired man, one who spoke with authority, and "not as the scribes."

Henri was so authentic in his dealings with people, and so gripping as a speaker and writer, that he did indeed remind many people of Jesus. The regular rules somehow got suspended when Henri Nouwen was around, and anything seemed possible. He created an atmosphere in his classes and before an audience that was open and receptive to the Spirit. Everything was done in a special, inspired way. His classes at Yale were punctuated regularly by songs. Nouwen would lead the class in a song, then speak for a while, then lead the class in singing another song. By the end, everyone had quite forgotten that they were at Yale University, taking a class for credit. They had left all that far behind.

Everywhere he spoke, his tone was that of a retreat director giving a spiritual conference. But instead of keeping to the measured tones of someone leading a quiet retreat, he would build to a crescendo of energy and inspiration on stage, waving his arms and arching up onto his tiptoes. As a speaker and teacher he showed himself a true master and he had that rare commodity—a true message.

Vincent van Gogh

Van Gogh, Self-Portrait. (Paris, Musée d'Orsay)

Most people know Vincent van Gogh to have been a very emotional Impressionist painter, one who created a body of work of such vivid color and beauty that he is now considered one of the most popular visual artists of the world. Henri Nouwen became fascinated by Vincent van Gogh, but his interest went beyond his personality or his output as a painter. Nouwen's interpretation of van Gogh focused on van Gogh's spiritual significance. Henri Nouwen studied van Gogh's art, his letters, and his biography and came to the conclusion that Vincent was a uniquely valuable witness to the agony and the ecstasy that are part of an authentic search for God.

Like Henri, van Gogh was a Dutchman, and their origins and life experience were similar in other respects as well. Vincent's father was a Protestant pastor and Vincent's first forays into the world were also in the role of a minister. He attended theological school and went on a mission to preach the gospel to the poor working in the mines of Belgium. Later, Vincent went through a mystical phase in which the reading and interpretation of Scripture were his chief interest. Even later, when he turned wholeheartedly to painting, he never relinquished his calling as a minister.

Van Gogh, like Nouwen, was a passionate seeker who quested after ideals that others may have regarded as unattainable. Different from other people, he was socially inept and often made people feel uncomfortable. He held strong views on many topics, such as nature and the proper way to depict religious topics in art. Although alive with spiritual concern, he

"I experienced connections between Vincent's struggle and my own, and realized more and more that Vincent was becoming my wounded healer. He painted what I had not before dared to look at; he questioned what I had not before dared to speak about; and he entered into the spaces of my heart that I had not dared to come close to."
—*Foreword to Cliff Edwards,* **Van Gogh and God**

avoided painting biblical scenes and other traditional religious subjects, because these were based on the artist's imagination, rather than observation of God's world. Instead, in his landscapes and portraits he brought to life a vision of a world that is transfused with God's presence and transformed into a new reality. Instead of angels and martyrs, the skies above might churn with evocative cloud formations; in his portraits a woman's forehead and cheeks could be blocked out in a vivid green or red, and the sunflowers and cypresses of the fields could burst into dancing movement on his glorious canvases. Henri found all of this both fascinating and significant. Vincent became a standard against which he measured other artists, as he does in this passage he wrote regarding the paintings of Edward Hopper:

> It is amazing to see . . . how close the connections are between the artistic work and the life and personality of the artist. This certainly is the case with all the artists I have paid attention to: Rembrandt, van Gogh, and Chagall. Edward Hopper's chilling life, frightfully reflected in his chilling art, affirms this connection. Vincent van Gogh's relationships were not any more satisfying than Hopper's. But there is a huge difference between the two. Vincent's fervent desire to be close to somebody, his dream of forming a colony of artists, and, most of all, his affectionate although turbulent love for his brother, Theo, is visible in all his works. In contrast to that of Hopper, Vincent's light is not only brilliant, but full of warmth. All the people he paints are radiant like saints, and his orchids, cypresses, and wheat fields are burning with the fire of his intense feelings. His many hot yellows are radically different from the cold yellows of Edward Hopper. The soul of the artist cannot remain hidden. The bitter, isolated, and mean soul of Hopper and the restless but love-hungry soul of van Gogh are both revealed in their works. Vincent van Gogh was and remained a minister, always trying to bring people together, even though he failed miserably. Edward Hopper was and remained a man who was only interested in himself, and he lived and died in splendid isolation. [13]

"Dear Lord, I will remain restless, tense, and dissatisfied until I can be totally at peace in your house. . . . With Vincent van Gogh, I keep asking your angel, whom I meet on the road, 'Does the road go uphill then all the way?' And the answer is, 'Yes, to the very end.' And I ask again: 'And will the journey take all day long?' And the answer is: 'From morning till night, my friend.'"

—A Cry for Mercy

For Henri Nouwen, Vincent was always a minister. While teaching at Yale Divinity School, Henri offered a spirituality class called "The Ministry of Vincent van Gogh" that both he and many of his students deemed the deepest, most effective class of his career there. He felt he had so much to share about Vincent in those years that Henri began to tour around, performing a monologue in which he appeared with one of his ears bandaged and spoke in Vincent's "voice." There is a very funny story told about his visit to a group of nuns who watched his Vincent performance in confusion and even horror. When he had a chance to ask the organizer what was wrong, she told him, "When we asked you to come give our keynote address about Vincent, we were actually referring to our founder, St. Vincent de Paul!" [14]

Henri Nouwen had a special ability for meditating on subjects and finding their spiritual significance. In Vincent van Gogh he saw a similar focus and meditative spirit, a sincere yearning and true insight into God's presence in the world. God was in the fields, in the alleyways, in the glance of an old seaman or the tilted sunbonnet of a faded beauty. This was a zenlike vision, and in fact Vincent owed as much to Japanese models as to European ones. This vision made a profound impact on Nouwen's own way of viewing the world. Henri made a deep and lasting connection to Vincent, his earlier countryman. Henri and Vincent were soulmates, and Henri called Vincent "one of the main spiritual guides of my life." [15]

Van Gogh, Old Man in Sorrow.
(Otterlo, Rijksmuseum Kröller-Muller)

A Troubled Heart,
an Artistic Temperament

The deep affinity that Henri Nouwen felt for Vincent van Gogh may have been due partly to a similarity in their temperaments. Like Vincent, Henri can be said to have had the same artistic, visionary or contemplative view of the world, and he dealt creatively and deeply with any of the subjects that he engaged in his writing. However, like Vincent, Henri was also a troubled man, someone whose sensitivity could become a two-edged sword. Certainly it opened up new vistas to him, but on the other hand, it sometimes drove him to anxious despair.

(Photo by Stephen Larson. Courtesy Photograph Series, Henri Nouwen Archives)

Because of these two sides to his personality, many have called Henri a complex figure. To many of his friends it seemed strange that someone so productive and inspired could at the same time be seized with terrible doubts and fears. One of Henri's good friends, Borys Gudiak, even observed once, somewhat ruefully, that Henri, although a teacher of prayer and contemplation, often seemed to be on the verge of a nervous breakdown. It was true; Henri's own fluidity of feelings and intensity meant that he often found himself on a roller coaster ride from equilibrium to joy to turmoil.

The source of his very real anxiety is difficult to pinpoint, but it was most acute or most visible in his dealings with friends and family. He had a deep need for love and acceptance that no relationship seemed to satisfy. He also felt very insecure sometimes, even fearing that friends would forget him or just disappear from his life. He was even troubled by a nagging fear that no one would be present at his funeral.

One component of Henri's psychological issues was a real sense of shame, a feeling that there was something wrong with him that he couldn't correct. The origins of these feelings are obscure, but there was one factor that certainly exacerbated his sense of unworthiness: Henri was a gay man, and he grew up in a time and place in which this could not be acknowledged. Homosexuality was never discussed in his home, and Dutch society and Roman Catholicism were unanimous in regarding this sexual orientation as a mental illness, and the living out of it as a sin. Thus, Henri grew up believing that he was different from other people, and thinking that this difference was so terrible that it must be kept a secret. Celibacy kept the issue under wraps for the most part, but he eventually needed to come to grips with how he felt deep inside, and needed to decide if there was any way he could legitimately acknowledge his feelings.

As a writer Henri had slowly evolved toward an attitude of greater and greater vulnerability and openness. Instead of posing as an expert, Henri made himself an everyman. He joked

"What I am craving is not so much recognition, praise, or admiration, as simple friendship. There may be some around me, but I cannot perceive or receive it. Within me lies a deadness that leaves me cold, tired, and rigid. . . . I attended a small workshop about the basic meaning of being a Christian, but little of what was said reached my heart. I realized that the only thing I really wanted was a handshake, an embrace, a kiss, or a smile; I received none. Finally, I fell asleep in the late afternoon to escape it all."
—¡Gracias!

that his middle initials, J.M., stood for "just me." With increasing candor he set before his readers his many fears and anxieties, and he explained how God sometimes did, and sometimes did not comfort him in his distress. However, he never wrote about being gay. In fact, this was something that he shared with very few people while he was living in the United States. Several people he did confide in urged him to "come out," to tell everyone about his sexual identity, but he never did this. He felt that if he were to admit to being homosexual, then the rest of his message would immediately be lost from sight; he would be labeled as a gay priest, and everything he said about Jesus and the spiritual life from then on would be seen through that filter.

So what was to be done about his emotional ups and downs and his deep sense of unease? Henri slowly learned, and also taught his readers, to be more trusting and more open to God even in the midst of distress. In a world of bold and confident spiritual leaders, Henri acknowledged his weaknesses and found a more humble, Christ-like way to live and speak. Oddly enough, when he was honest about his feelings, his message became even more penetrating and important for his readers. In voicing his own doubts and distress, he apparently spoke for many. His readers decided that Henri was someone who felt just like they did, and they accepted his witness to his own predicament and his counsel with gratitude.

What do you do when you are always comparing yourself with other people? What do you do when you always feel that the people you talk to, hear of, or read about are more intelligent, more skillful, more attractive, more gentle, more generous, more practical, or more contemplative than you are? What do you do when you can't get away from measuring yourself against others, always feeling that they are the real people while you are a nobody or even less than that? . . . I talked about this with John Eudes today. . . . We talked about the vicious cycle one enters when one has a low self-esteem or self-doubt and then

---

"Come, Lord, break through my compulsions, anxieties, fears, and guilt feelings, and let me see my sin and your mercy. Amen."

—A Cry for Mercy

(Photo by Kevin Dwyer, used with permission)

perceives other people in such a way as to strengthen and confirm these feelings. It is the famous self-fulfilling prophesy all over again. I enter into relationships with some apprehension and fear and behave in such a way that whatever the others say or do, I experience them as stronger, better, more valuable persons, and myself as weaker, worse, and not worth talking to. After a while the relationship becomes intolerable. . . . John Eudes talked about that moment, that point, that spot that lies before the comparison, before the beginning of the vicious cycle or the self-fulfilling prophesy. That is the moment, point, or place where meditation can enter in. It is the moment to stop reading, speaking, socializing, and to "waste" your time in meditation. [16]

Latin America

As with most of Nouwen's interests, it is difficult to pinpoint when he first began to think about Latin America. However, as a European living in the United States, he came to realize that the American continent was made up of two zones or two realities—one northern and one southern. Yet it seemed just as clear to him that both realities were part of a single whole. Living in the America of the north, he became more and more curious as to what lay to the south, in the other, Latin half of the New World.

He had first begun to meet Catholics with ties to Latin America while at Notre Dame; these were both priests who had been to Latin America as missionaries and Latin Americans who had gone to Notre Dame to study. Once forged, these connections were maintained, and as Henri's restlessness began to come more and more to the surface while at Yale, and as his long romance with the Cistercians began to cool down, Henri began to ask himself if he ought to consider mission work in Latin America. He started to explore this possibility by traveling down to visit friends living in various Latin American countries, thus exploring a vast continent full of many lively and engaging people, and one with a deep religious and artistic tradition and a great need for cultural and material development.

In Latin America Henri found a type of Catholicism that shared many elements with the traditional European faith of his youth. But to that traditional, vivid sense of God's presence the Latin Americans added solidarity with the poor and a vision of a better world just about to be built. Latin America is all about hope in a better future. For someone with high religious ideals,

Latin America can seem irresistible, and Henri Nouwen was soon captivated. Suddenly the South couldn't wait, couldn't be confined to a sabbatical experience or a class topic that he presented at Yale University. He decided that ten years at Yale were enough, and that he wanted more than anything else to commit himself to mission in Latin America. In his mind, this was not a sudden or a radical departure, but something that had been taking shape for many years. He writes:

The question: "Does God call me to Latin America?" was not a new question for me. From the day I left Holland to teach pastoral theology at Yale Divinity School, I had been wondering about the connection between the northern and southern parts of the American continent. Somehow I felt that teaching future ministers in the United States about God's mysterious work with people could not be done unless the word "people" included the millions of Spanish- and Portuguese-speaking human beings whose destiny is intimately linked with that of their English-speaking brothers and sisters. Somehow, I knew that God's voice could not be heard unless it would include the voices of the men, women, and children of Latin America. [17]

"Can we truly live with the poor? Although I live with them and share their life to some extent, I am far from poor."
—¡Gracias!

In Lima, Peru, Nouwen lived with the Moreno family. (Courtesy Photograph Series, Henri Nouwen Archives)

In the Moreno house in Lima, Nouwen occupied a room on the roof. On the photograph he has written "My Penthouse." (Courtesy Photograph Series, Henri Nouwen Archives)

"My room consists of four brick walls—painted pink ('the only color I had') by our neighbor Octavio—and a roof made of sheets of metal. With virtually no rain here and with little cold weather, my small place seems quite comfortable and pleasant."

–¡Gracias!

So it was that Henri Nouwen resigned his position at Yale in 1981 and went first to the Abbey of the Genesee to take stock of the situation and make some concrete preparations. After doing some research and talking to friends and advisors he was ultimately invited to become an associate of the Maryknoll order in their work and mission in Peru. Although Peru would be his base, it was suggested that he go first to a Spanish language school run by Maryknoll in neighboring Bolivia. The whole trial period would last six months, with half spent in school and half in the mission field.

Of course, he kept a journal. It is full of impressions of the kaleidoscopic contrast between the terrible and the wonderful sides to living in the South. Nouwen's time in Latin America was for him an emotional roller coaster of intense experiences. He saw that the poverty and violence that endures there can be swallowed up in expressions of joy and of humanity that our middle-class world seems to have long ago abandoned. He was struck over and over again with the simplicity and generosity of the people he met.

Henri was there to discern his path, and he did so in typical Nouwen fashion, by diving into the life of the people and into dozens of new friendships, all the while writing away and recording his experience. The book that would emerge from this "journal of discernment" was called *¡Gracias!*

In the latter half of his trial period he lived with several families in a *barrio nuevo,* a shantytown in Lima. Being in Peru was an inspiring experience. Not only was he able to make concrete, rather than abstract, his sense of what Latin American poverty was and was not, he came to know some of the leading figures in the liberation theology movement, especially Gustavo Gutiérrez, its leading exponent. Gutiérrez was Nouwen's guide to the theology of the South, and he couldn't have asked for a better mentor. However, it became apparent to Gutiérrez and perhaps to others that Henri Nouwen was not someone who should make a lasting commitment to Latin America. It was suggested that he might be more useful if he were to return to the United States and explain to people there what was happening

"Today I became fifty years old. I am glad that I can celebrate this birthday in the parish of Ciudad de Dios and with my family in Pamplona Alta. I hope that by concluding here half a century of living, I am perhaps moving toward a new way of living and working in the future."
—¡Gracias!

The Maryknoll parish of Ciudad de Dios in Lima, Peru.
(Maryknoll archives)

Cover of ¡Gracias! A Latin American Journal *(Harper & Row, 1983).*

"The plane from Buenos Aires and Santiago has just arrived. I am eager to get on board and head north; but I am also aware that something has happened to me. I sit here and wonder if going north still means going home."

—¡Gracias!

in Latin America, and thus be a bridge between these two worlds. Henri should not stay in Latin America, but he could do the work of "reverse mission" in the North.

Henri Nouwen accepted this judgment and returned to the United States, but he did not return unchanged or empty-handed. He knew that he had been right about America being one single reality, and that much work needed to be done in the North if the North were ever to receive the gift of the South. Just as Henri left the monastery but managed to take the monastery with him, so he left Latin America very much aware that Latin America would be part of his life in many ways from that point forward. He expressed some of that new perspective in this reflection:

The spirituality of liberation touches every dimension of life. It is a truly biblical spirituality that allows God's saving act in history to penetrate all levels of human existence. God is seen here as the God of the living who enters into humanity's history to dispel the forces of death, wherever they are at work, and to call forth the healing and rec-onciling forces of life. . . . With this new self-consciousness, the poor have broken into history and have rediscovered that the God whom they have worshipped for centuries is not a God who wants their poverty but a God who wants to liberate them from those forces of death and offer them life in all its dimensions. [18]

A New Agenda

Arriving back in the United States, Henri Nouwen returned to the residence at the Genesee monastery that had been his base prior to making his Latin American pilgrimage. He put out a feeler to Harvard Divinity School, one which Harvard eagerly followed up by offering him a position. Nouwen then demurred, saying he did not want to engage in university teaching full time. After some correspondence back and forth it was agreed that Nouwen would go to Harvard, but he would teach only one semester each year, being free the second semester to pursue other interests.

Evidently there were many other interests. The books that Nouwen published in this period are quite varied, from his *¡Gracias!* journal at one end to *Behold the Beauty of the Lord,* a

Henri with young friends in Santiago Atitlan, Guatemala, September 1984. (Photo by Peter Weiskel, used with permission)

Henri with Father John Vesey in front of the parish church of Santiago Atitlan. The previous pastor, Fr. Stanley Rother, had been murdered by death squads in 1981.
(Photo by Peter Weiskel, used with permission)

book on praying with icons, at the other. Yet Nouwen wanted most to fulfill his promise and do a serious tour of public speaking and other networking in order to raise the consciousness of people living in the United States about Latin America. Harvard would be a good public platform from which he could carry out this plan.

These were the years of the Reagan administration, and there was a struggle going on in the United States over whether Latin America should be seen as an area in need of solidarity and material support, or as a staging ground for a communist takeover of North America. Today the threat of communism seems *passé,* but not at that time. In those years some conservative commentators were even calculating in public how many hours it would take for a band of revolutionaries to drive from Nicaragua, then under the Sandinista government, to the Texas border.

To counter this "threat," the American government was funding repressive regimes in El Salvador and Guatemala, and private armies known as Contras that were trying to bring down the Nicaraguan government. However, this funding was controversial. The majority of better-informed Americans knew that the Contras were involved in terrorizing the rural poor and killing, raping, and driving into exile the indigenous population. Trying to stop the armed conflict raging in Central America was the prime factor motivating Nouwen's efforts when he returned to speak as widely as possible on Latin America and to meet personally with senators and congressmen in Washington. In so doing, he sought to dispel some of the fear and misinformation that was being used to justify the funding of the right-wing terrorists.

In typical Nouwen fashion, Henri did not attack the American cold-war mentality directly or mount intellectual arguments. Instead, he talked about his experiences in Latin America, about the human cost of poverty and conflict in Central America, and about the need for spiritual solidarity between the North and the South. He talked to people about people, and did what he could to sway those few who would listen, if not public opinion in general. The following quotation gives a sense of Nouwen's message to the North:

> *"If I have any vocation in Latin America, it is the vocation to receive from the people the gifts they have to offer us and to bring these gifts back up north for our own conversion and healing."*
> —¡Gracias!

As we see the increasing violence in Central America, that inflamed cord that binds the two continents together, we must humbly confess that something more than political conflict is happening there. It is a deeply spiritual crisis that involves both Americas, North and South. It is a crisis that reveals the failure of five centuries of Christianity to bring unity to the Americas. The oppression, violence, and mass murder that ravage El Salvador and Guatemala remind us that we are crucifying Christ again. But his death among us is also a "kairos," an opportunity for conversion. [19]

Blessed Are the Peacemakers

"One of the reasons why so many people have developed strong reservations about the peace movement is precisely that they do not see the peace they seek in the peacemakers themselves."

—Peacework

For many people, being "spiritual" is understood as a personal deepening that requires a certain distance from the mad clamor of the world, and they are right. However, a true spirituality cannot ignore or forget the issues that convulse our society or the pleas for justice from the many victims of wrongdoing who live in our world. Henri Nouwen recognized this and struggled during his life to find the best way to express his position on the important social issues of his day. Although he was by this point very well known for his writings on personal spirituality, a commitment to social justice was becoming a big part of his life, a part that most people do not realize was so significant.

Besides Henri's efforts to change American attitudes and policy towards Central America, he was active in a number of other causes. The first of these, the civil rights movement, had impacted him years earlier. Henri took part in civil rights marches in the American South and wrote about these experiences, primarily for interested readers in Holland.

Later, when teaching at Yale, he found himself in a university environment that was shaken and polarized by opposition to the Vietnam War and divided over a host of cultural issues. Henri's reaction to the counterculture protestors and student activists on campus was more ambivalent than the way he felt about the civil rights movement. He might agree with some of their concerns, but he disliked their methods and could not respect their often disorderly and irresponsible lifestyles. His ideal with regard to social justice, as well as spirituality, was Thomas Merton, who had seen peacemaking as a high and exacting calling. One of Merton's famous dictums was: "Peace demands the most heroic labor and the most difficult sacrifice. It demands greater heroism than war. It demands greater fidelity to the truth and a much more perfect purity of conscience." This disciplined, spiritual approach to peace was not displayed by many in the frenzy of the counterculture period.

Although he could not identify with the protest movement generally, at Yale he met a number of deeply principled and religious people who were involved in acts of civil disobedience. One of these was Dean Hammer, a Jew and a Ploughshares activist who was repeatedly arrested and jailed for taking part in provocative demonstrations at antinuclear protests. He also began to correspond with John Dear, a Jesuit who was very active in peace and justice work, and who was also frequently in jail, and this led to a long and important friendship. Through these and similar contacts, Henri began to support and then to take part in protests himself, primarily against nuclear weapons. Since nearby Groton, Connecticut, was home to Electric Boat, the firm that manufactured the deadly Trident nuclear submarine, this weapon system was one focus of his attention.

Good Friday Stations of the Cross becomes a march for peace in New Haven, 1985. (Courtesy Henri Nouwen Literary Centre)

Later Henri also became involved in responding to the AIDS epidemic. As the epidemic brought sickness and death to increasing numbers of gay men in the United States and Europe, Nouwen was drawn into their suffering and some of his ambivalence about the gay lifestyle began to evaporate. He was moved to see a lifestyle he had sometimes criticized in more positive and humane terms, and part of this movement in his thinking included greater acceptance of his own sexuality. The compassion he felt for stricken and dying gay Christians led him to be less judgmental and reconsider the value of their witness to the church. He ultimately decided that "homosexual people had a unique vocation in the Christian community."[20] This became another social issue that he felt cried out for justice and redress.

Nouwen's *Peacework, written in 1981, was first published in 2005 (Orbis).*

"Peacemaking can no longer be regarded as peripheral to being a Christian. It is not something like joining the parish choir. Nobody can be a Christian without being a peacemaker."

—Peacework

The civil rights movement, Latin America, nuclear disarmament, the AIDS epidemic—these were the causes that interested Henri the most. He wrote, visited activists, spoke out, and even took part in protests throughout his life, yet many of his friends thought he should do more. They urged him to take a stronger stance and capitalize on his national reputation to draw attention to one cause or another and help bring about real change. In fact, as Henri regarded the motley array of activists agitating for this and against that, he sometimes found it difficult to identify completely with them or their causes. Their own positions were often reactive, angry and fearful, full of the same impulses and emotions as those of the people they opposed.

Henri Nouwen knew in his heart that a different approach was needed. He ultimately proposed a spirituality of peacemaking that began by realigning oneself with God in prayer and renouncing the world's message of negativity, self-criticism, fearfulness, and violence. He unmasked as lunacy the quest to obtain one's own national security by threatening the survival of humanity. However, he also attacked those who sit as passive bystanders merely watching the arms race or U.S.-sponsored regional conflicts, saying that such people did not understand the implications of the gospel. What he himself envisioned was a spirituality of peace and peacemaking that was grounded in prayer, self-knowledge, mutuality, and love for one's enemies.

Nouwen's message regarding peacemaking was not as widely heard as some of his other insights. Some of this was due to his own quiet approach to this issue. He came to believe that spending the afternoon visiting the sick could contribute to God's peace just as much as going to a rally for nuclear disarmament, or perhaps even more. Indeed, although he wrote a book laying out a spirituality of peacemaking, he never published it during his lifetime. This very mature and penetrating work only appeared in 2005. It has a foreword written by John Dear and is entitled *Peacework: Prayer, Resistance, Community.* Fr. Dear had earlier gathered a posthumous collection of Nouwen

Nouwen preaching at a Witness for Peace ecumenical worship service in Cambridge, Massachusetts, 1984.
(Photo by Peter Weiskel, used with permission)

writings on peace and social justice, including an excerpt from this same *Peacework*, called *The Road to Peace*. These writings reveal that peace and social justice, although a lesser-known side of Henri Nouwen's vision, are nevertheless essential elements. Nouwen's balanced, holistic vision of peacework asks that anyone hoping to be a saint be a peacemaker, and anyone hoping to be a peacemaker be a saint. The two are inextricably bound together:

> *Visiting the sick, feeding the hungry, consoling the dying, or sheltering the homeless may not catch the public eye and are often perceived as irrelevant when put in the perspective of a possible nuclear holocaust. There are many voices who say: "These little acts of mercy are a waste of time when we consider the urgency of stopping the arms race." But the peacemaker knows that true peace is a divine gift which has nothing to do with statistics or measures of success and popularity. Peace is like life itself. It manifests itself quietly and gently. Who can say that a "lost afternoon" with a sick friend is in truth not much more than an interruption of "true" peacework? It might be the most real contribution to peace. Who knows? Jesus' way is the humble way. He calls out to us: "Learn from me for I am gentle and humble of heart" (Matt. 11:29). A humble "Yes" to all forms of life—even the less noticed— affirms the deep interconnection between all people and forms the true basis of peace.* [21]

"Could it be possible that the pain and struggles of the North American people are an intimate part of the pains and struggles of the people of South America?"
—The Road to Peace

Harvard

Harvard Divinity School. (Courtesy Harvard Divinity School)

After ten years spent teaching at Yale, one might assume that Henri Nouwen would be able to adapt fairly easily to Harvard, a sister Ivy League institution with an equally prestigious reputation. However, the culture and ambience of the two schools are in ways very different. Harvard University is physically much larger than Yale, and is part of greater Boston, one of the major urban areas of the United States. Yale strikes the visitor as quieter, somewhat more traditional, and more private than Harvard, which can seem at times like a clamorous public market for theories and ideas, a university with more currents from more sources than Yale. Most importantly, Harvard Divinity School is Unitarian in its origins, and attracts students and faculty with a much wider range of backgrounds and beliefs than Yale Divinity School, which is much more clearly a Christian divinity school.

Henri Nouwen arrived at Harvard with an open mind and a determination to understand what this great university was all about. In his first period there he attended classes and lectures given by other divinity school faculty and made overtures of friendship to several of them. He wanted to make friends and he himself wanted to teach a class that combined everything he had learned on his journey, a class that he entitled "An Introduction to the Spiritual Life." Of course, his fame had preceded him, and the class he taught was mobbed with students from Harvard and from surrounding seminaries. Everyone wanted to hear what Henri Nouwen had to say.

In the face of these great expectations, and taking the Gospel of Luke as his text, Henri wove together his vision of

Lecturing at Harvard Divinity School. (Courtesy Photograph Series, Henri Nouwen Archives)

the spiritual life, a vision that combined monasticism, prayer, politics, Latin America, and much more, yet his Harvard experience failed to satisfy him. Part of his unhappiness stemmed from how he was being perceived. In the pluralistic atmosphere that is Harvard Divinity School, Henri Nouwen, the great Christian risk-taker, seemed like a traditionalist. Furthermore, in reaching out to the people at Harvard, he realized he was trying too hard and adapting too much.

Returning to Harvard for a second year of teaching after being gone almost a year, Henri Nouwen felt the need to be more straightforward about Jesus, who should obviously be at the heart of Christian spirituality. Between sessions at Harvard he had thought a lot about Jesus and was sure he had to be more direct when speaking to his Harvard students. He also felt he had some important things to say. His vision, especially after Latin America, was of Jesus as God come down from heaven— Jesus as the descending God who penetrated to the lowest level of human poverty and earthly existence.

For this second class he chose as his text the Gospel of John, the most radical and uncompromising of the four Christian Gospels, and choosing this text produced an imme-

Altar in Henri Nouwen's Cambridge apartment. (Photo by Mary Carney, used with permission)

"*I had the feeling that Harvard was not where God wanted me to be. It's too much podium, too much publicity, too public. Too many people came to listen. . . . It's not an intimate place. It's a place of intellectual battle.*"

—The Road to Peace

diate change in the tone of the class. Henri kept the focus on the gospel, on Jesus, and on what he referred to as "the descending way" that Jesus called believers to embrace. The reaction among the students was mixed. Those who had come into Harvard from the Catholic and Evangelical schools in the area embraced what Henri was saying with gratitude, but the emphasis on Jesus and Henri's own more uncompromising stance scandalized many of the Harvard students, who were unaccustomed to hearing anyone speak about Jesus with such authority. They accused Henri of "spiritual imperialism" and of ignoring other minority and nontraditional approaches to spirituality in favor of something unilateral and arrogant.

Henri was mystified and hurt that he was being so completely misunderstood. He tried to make changes and be more "inclusive," but by this point no one was satisfied. Henri began to sink into a depression and to feel more and more uncomfortable at Harvard. He had hoped to make this great school a platform to tell more and more people about Latin America. He had ended up speaking out about Jesus and spirituality, but this approach was not working. Many wonderful people were visiting him and he made some important friends in the area, but Harvard Divinity School was not a good place for him, and he knew he would have to leave. Later he would reflect,

My decision to leave Harvard was a difficult one. For many months I was not sure if I would be following or betraying my vocation by leaving. The outer voices kept saying, "You can do so much good here. People need you!" The inner voices kept saying, "What good is it to preach the Gospel to others while losing your own soul?" Finally, I realized that my increasing inner darkness, my feelings of being rejected by some of my students, colleagues, friends, and even God, my inordinate need for affirmation and affection, and my deep sense of not belonging were clear signs that I was not following the way of God's spirit. . . . I feel no regrets about my time at Harvard. Though in a divinity school, I had a real chance to be in a thoroughly secular

At Harvard with Professor Harvey Cox and long-time friend Richard White, 1984. (Photo by Peter Weiskel)

university environment, and I had the opportunity to experience joy and fear in speaking directly about Jesus. [22]

As this quotation clearly shows, Henri Nouwen felt confused and disappointed by his time at Harvard. He had clung to the Gospel of John and been treated to some of the rejection that that Gospel speaks about. He himself felt caught on the descending way that he had made a central part of his message, and he hoped that Jesus was with him as he plunged first into depression and then off the academic stage.

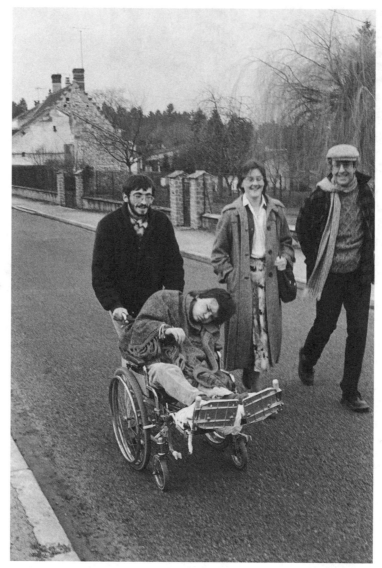

Walking with L'Arche community members in Trosly-Breuil, December 1985. (Photo by Peter Weiskel, used with permission)

Trosly

etween the two semesters Henri Nouwen taught at Harvard, he went to France for a thirty-day retreat in Trosly, a village that is home to Jean Vanier and the l'Arche community. Nine months later, when he finished teaching, he returned to this community, this time for a longer stay. He had a feeling that this new direction he was embarking on had been many years in the making. It began long ago when Nouwen, in his book *Clowning in Rome,* mentioned Jean Vanier as someone whom he greatly admired but had never met. Vanier subsequently asked a friend of his to pay a visit to Nouwen and then invited Henri to join him on a silent retreat in Chicago. Vanier sensed how lost he was feeling and invited him to "spend a year" with him at Trosly. Frankly, Jean Vanier thought that the l'Arche community could give Henri what he

Henri in Rome with Jean Vanier.
(Courtesy Henri Nouwen Literary Centre)

needed, which was a spiritual home. When Henri arrived in Trosly for the second time, it was to spend an entire year with Vanier and with l'Arche.

Jean Vanier is a Swiss-born Canadian and the son of the very distinguished Georges Vanier, the former governor general of Canada. Georges and his wife Pauline led such exemplary lives of service and Christian witness, particularly during and after World War II, when they offered great assistance to refugees, that they are now being considered for beatification by the Catholic Church.

After obtaining a doctorate in philosophy in Paris, their son Jean taught in Toronto, then abandoned academia and joined his spiritual director, Père Thomas Philippe, in Trosly. There he set up a residence in a small house. To this residence he brought two mentally handicapped men from a nearby institution where Père Thomas worked in order to live in long-term solidarity with them. He called the foyer he established l'Arche, which is French for "the ark." Soon other handicapped men and women arrived, as did young volunteers who agreed to live with and assist them for a year or more.

Thus, from a small gesture of hospitality and solidarity was born an international movement that now numbers more than one hundred communities around the world. L'Arche is set up as an ecumenical community, but the sensitive spirituality of French Catholicism is a very strong component of the Trosly community. From its French origins comes its sacramentality, a slower pace, an attention to small details and humble people, and a readiness to turn every meal and gathering into a celebration.

Jean Vanier and l'Arche were a revelation to Henri Nouwen. Here he saw put into practice many of the principles he had preached and championed for years—the downward mobility and solidarity of the young volunteers, the centrality of the Eucharist, the inclusion of the most marginalized members of society, and the recognition of God's grace working among and through these forgotten individuals. According to

"Jean Vanier, the Canadian who founded a worldwide network of communities for mentally disabled people, has remarked more than once that Jesus did not say: 'Blessed are those who care for the poor,' but 'Blessed are the poor.' Simple as this remark may seem, it offers the key to the kingdom."

—Here and Now

Saying Mass with Père Thomas at a wedding at Trosly-Breuil.
(Photo courtesy John and Joelle Peeters)

"Life at l'Arche is built upon love, not simply for handicapped people, but for the God of life revealed to us in Jesus Christ, the rejected man of Nazareth."
—The Road to Daybreak

Henri, l'Arche was a community living in the true spirit of Jesus, in the spirit of the Beatitudes.

During his long stay in Trosly Henri took an active part in community life, resided in the home of Madame Vanier, Jean Vanier's exemplary mother, and took advantage of the opportunity to consult Jean Vanier and his mentor, Père Thomas, people whose work he admired and whose philosophy he realized he shared. Peter Weiskel, who visited Nouwen at Trosly, has said that Jean Vanier was like an older brother in Christ for Henri Nouwen. Indeed, this was a very important relationship

With Madame Vanier, Jean's mother. (Courtesy Photograph Series, Henri Nouwen Archives)

for Henri. It was also true that l'Arche seemed to meet many of Nouwen's needs for support and for community.

Here was a place that accepted everyone just as they were. Henri realized that he had been looking for years for somewhere he could be accepted for who he was, an acceptance that was unrelated to his success and fame as an author and spiritual authority. The l'Arche core members, as the disabled members of the community were known, gave him a warm person-to-person welcome that was profoundly important for him, especially because they had no idea who Henri Nouwen was.

Henri describes an evening service at Trosly in these words:

During evening prayer we sang simple songs, we listened to Danny, one of the handicapped men from Cork, who with great difficulty read from Jean Vanier's book, I Meet Jesus, *and we prayed. Danny said, "I love you, Jesus. I do not reject you even when I get nervous once in a while . . . even when I get confused. I love you with my arms, my legs, my head, my heart; I love you and I do not reject you, Jesus. I know that you love me, that you love me so much. I love you too, Jesus."* . . . *I suddenly felt a deep desire to invite all my students from Harvard to sit with me there in that circle. I felt a deep love for all those men and women I had tried to speak to about Jesus and had often failed to touch. I wanted so much for all of them to sit and let Danny tell them about Jesus. I knew they would understand what I had not been able to explain.* [23]

During his long stay at Trosly Henri made a brief visit to Toronto to serve as celebrant at the wedding of a friend. He asked permission to stay at the Toronto l'Arche community while he was there and hoped that the isolation would enable him to do some writing. Events, however, took a different turn. While staying at Daybreak, as the community north of Toronto is known, an accident took place that threw the community into turmoil. Raymond, a core member, was hit by car and seriously injured. Moreover, to his parents, the Daybreak community seemed partly to blame. Raymond was in intensive care and seemed to be on the point of dying. Seeing how devastated everyone was by this crisis, Henri stepped forward to provide pastoral guidance to the community, restored calm, and helped reconcile the community and the family. This intervention had a profound impact on the Daybreak community. They were so moved by the way that Henri had ministered to them that once he was gone, they composed a letter to him asking that he return to serve as their pastor.

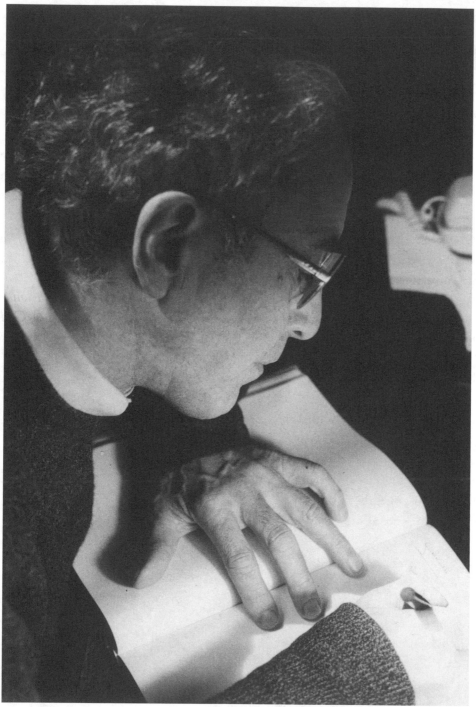

(Photo by Kevin Dwyer, used with permission)

Letters to Marc about Jesus

Although Henri Nouwen was almost uniquely able to make connections to Jesus as part of whatever he was then talking about, he never wrote the big book about Jesus and the Gospels many expected him to write. However, while staying at Trosly he wrote a series of letters, in part for publication, and in part to his nephew Marc, and these letters provide an important outline of what Henri thought about the role of Jesus in the lives of modern people. *Letters to Marc* is subtitled, *Living a Spiritual Life in a Material World*. It is one of only a small handful of books that Henri Nouwen wrote in his native language.

In *Letters to Marc* Nouwen defines spiritual living as an awareness of the heart of existence, and asks what Jesus has to do with that. He explains that Jesus, by transcending the brutality and deadly violence of his own life, and by offering new life to his friends, became a God who sets captives free. This liberation is tied in a special way to the Eucharist, which is a ritual that brings us face-to-face with Christ's death and resurrection. As we consider the story of his death, we may be surprised to find that Christ approached the end of his life with great awareness and purpose. Through it he made God a partner in human suffering and brought God's compassion to humanity. This is important, because compassion is the path of freedom. God frees us, not by removing suffering from our lives, but by sharing it with us.

To illustrate the love of God, as shown in the life of Jesus, Henri tells Marc the story of Jean Vanier and l'Arche. It is the

"In the gospel it is quite obvious that Jesus chose the descending way. He chose it not once but over and over again. . . . When, finally, Jesus is hanging on the cross and cries out with a loud voice: 'My God, my God, why have you forsaken me?' only then do we know how far God has gone to show us his love."

—Letters to Marc about Jesus

tale of a man who turned aside from an aristocratic lifestyle and an elite education to embrace the poverty of those with mental disabilities. From his decision came a worldwide spiritual movement, one that Henri saw as a sign of God's love in the world. Christ is the exemplar of this kind of descent from exaltation to solidarity with those who suffer and are in need of redemption. "Descending" is the *leitmotif* of the gospel, the way of Christ and the way of all Christians, one in which we seek solidarity and find joy.

The gospel of Jesus plays out in a very personal way. We search the world over for anyone or anything that can calm our anxiety and provide us with a sense of our own worth and belovedness, yet seldom do we find what we seek. It is in Jesus, more than anywhere else, that we can find expressed the love that we need, for Jesus offers a love that is a transcendent force. It is not a love reserved for friends or for those who are worthy, but a love lavished on good and bad, friend and foe alike. It is in the Eucharist that this love is expressed for us most concretely.

Finally, Nouwen presents for Marc the case of a French mystic, Marthe Robin, who lived a life completely caught up in the suffering of Christ, and who yet remained hidden from the world. Nouwen sees this as a perfect example of how God chooses the small, obscure, and forgotten people of this world with whom to forge his closest friendships. The way of Jesus is a hidden way, for Jesus himself embraced a life that was not one of exaltation or power, but one of meekness and humility.

This was an important piece of writing for Henri Nouwen. In it we see him returning to Jesus and finding his center in the Lord. This return to the center stripped him of some false concepts that he had been harboring, as he noted in his summary:

> *In the course of writing I've discovered for myself the great extent to which I'm inclined to "secularize" Jesus. Instinctively, I look to Jesus for a cheap liberation, a solution to my problems, help with my desire*

Jean Vanier visiting Henri's lecture course on spirituality at Harvard, 1984. (Photo by Peter Weiskel, used with permission)

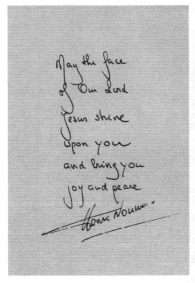

Icon of the Savior of Zvenigorad, one of Henri's favorites. The inscription reads: "May the face of Our Lord Jesus shine upon you and bring you joy and peace."

for success, getting even with my opponents, and a good measure of publicity. It's not always easy to see Jesus as the gospel presents him: as the Lord who calls us to spiritual freedom, shares our suffering, shows us the descending way, challenges us to love our enemies, and secretly reveals God's love to us. And yet, each time I catch a glimpse of the real Jesus, I'm conscious of a new inward peace, and it is again possible to recognize his voice and follow it. [24]

Canada

"Yesterday I received a long letter from Daybreak in Canada inviting me to join their community. . . . I am deeply moved by this letter. It is the first time in my life that I have been explicitly called. . . . It is a concrete call to follow Christ, to leave the world of success, accomplishment, and honor, and to trust Jesus and him alone."

—The Road to Daybreak

fter he had returned to Trosly, Henri Nouwen received the offer from Daybreak to join their community. Of all the requests and offers of employment he had received during his career, he was especially moved by the Daybreak letter, and asked himself if he should regard it as a call from God. He felt that no one had ever "called" him to a job in the same way before.

This was an open-ended time in Nouwen's life. Since leaving Yale several years earlier Henri had had more freedom to travel and follow his own interests and inclinations, but this greater level of freedom had left him feeling rootless and had exacerbated his uneasy feelings of shame and self-doubt. Neither Yale, nor Harvard, nor monasticism, nor the Latin American mission fields had been the right fit for him. He wanted to be more than just a writer of spiritual books, but could not find a suitable place for himself. He was looking for a ministry that would also provide him with a spiritual home, but, frankly, he was running out of options.

Daybreak had made him an interesting offer, but becoming a permanent part of l'Arche and moving to Toronto seemed so counterintuitive! First of all, he had to wonder if God could be calling him to something for which he had no talent. Although he had a niece who was disabled, he had no background in this area and had never considered working with the disabled as a ministry he might choose. In addition, he was . . . well, he was Henri Nouwen! He had many unique abilities and a phenomenal background. Would God call him to something so foreign for which he had no training or inter-

est when he had so much to offer in other areas? Essentially, going to Daybreak was not his idea, and it took him some time to decide that perhaps this was God's answer to his prayer.

When he did ultimately decide to accept the offer from Daybreak, one important factor was that a special Canadian friend he met at Trosly, Nathan Ball, was going to Toronto to study theology, and he would be living at Daybreak, too. As Nouwen reasoned, "I am not going alone." His friendship with Nathan had been one of the high points of his time in Trosly, and he looked forward to continuing to deepen this warm relationship in Toronto and face the new challenges with a close friend at his side.

So it was that Nouwen found himself leading a caravan of vehicles carrying his furniture and a number of friends north from Boston to Toronto, stopping at the Abbey of the Genesee on the way. His arrival at Daybreak with an entourage of vehicles was remembered years later by the Daybreak community as the

first of Nouwen's crazy surprises; after all, most people walked
into Daybreak carrying everything they needed in a small bag.

After his arrival came the process of slowing the energetic
Henri Nouwen down. As usual, he was flying high, full of
energy and plans to get off the treadmill of success, but at the
same time thinking that he was going to "offer classes" at
Daybreak. The community urged him to slow down, collect
himself, and learn about the community first. One of those
who watched his arrival with amusement was Mary Bastedo:

> *In September 1986, as I was pushing Adam Arnett in his wheel-
> chair to the day program, a big yellow moving van full of Henri's pos-
> sessions pulled in. Most assistants arrive with a backpack and a few
> possessions; here was a professor from Harvard arriving with all of this!
> Hence the raised eyebrows. Some of us had met Henri during his ear-
> lier visit. It was clear that he hardly knew how to make toast and tea,
> yet he was going to be a house assistant in the New House. Henri had
> purchased a brand-new car and was driving with his soon-to-be head
> of house, talking excitedly about how he just wanted to live a normal
> life. Suddenly they crashed into the car ahead. "This is not normal!"
> the head of house commented. And Henri had to buy a new car.* [25]

Back to Basics

Totaling his brand-new car was emblematic of the larg-er crash landing that Henri Nouwen made by moving to Toronto. It was an enormous adjustment for him to join the Daybreak community, even greater than entering the monastery or being in the Latin American mission fields. At least in those places he could exercise his familiar priestly role and focus on writing. Not in Toronto. Although Henri had been called to be the pastor of the Daybreak community, it was felt that he could not truly connect to the core members and the volunteers if he had not himself experienced the unique life that they were engaged in living.

Henri at Daybreak, with core member Bill van Buren, Carol Berry and her son, Kristof. (Courtesy Henri Nouwen Literary Centre)

(Nouwen family albums)

"Since nobody could read my books, they could not impress anyone, and since most of them never went to school, my twenty years at Notre Dame, Yale, and Harvard did not provide a significant introduction. . . . I was starting my life all over again."

—In the Name of Jesus

So it was that Henri Nouwen, at fifty-four years of age a cosmopolitan and cultured university professor, but admittedly a total incompetent when it came to simple practical matters (such as driving a car or making a meal), took up residence in the New House at Daybreak. It is a measure of his humility that he would agree to this type of basic training at his stage in life. Certainly this was not the first time he had been physically challenged: trying to be a monk had taxed him to his bodily limits, then Latin America had been altogether too rough for his tastes, but now he was to meet his worst challenge: living alongside the handicapped in a community where no one was exempt from doing the chores.

Living in the New House turned out to involve an endless round of making meals and cleaning up and caring for someone else. All of this was hard work. Henri also had great difficulty coordinating with the other community members regarding meals or other matters because of his very real impracticality. He never really grasped that you couldn't invite people to dinner without checking with the person doing the cooking, or any number of similar matters involving the physical and social facts of life.

One of the funniest stories that emerged from the New House relates how Henri and several others were caught up in a theological discussion while doing the dishes. The discussion went on and on, and so did the seemingly endless number of dishes to be washed. This chore was becoming truly lengthy and only came to an end when it was realized that Henri, while he was speaking and gesturing before his small audience of fellow dishwashers, was absent-mindedly picking up stacks of clean dishes and putting them back in the dirty dishwater to be washed over again!

Besides living in and taking part in the New House, Henri began converting another house into a retreat center and the basement of that building into a chapel. This, the Dayspring, would be his residence. The large plot of land where Daybreak

New House at Dayhreak. (Courtesy
Photograph Series, Henri Nouwen Archives)

was located had originally been a farm, and then had been a
convent occupied by a religious order. When Nouwen moved
there it still had a very rural character, with animals grazing in
the fields of the property. One of the farm buildings was used
as a woodshop that employed a number of core members. It
was real country living. Harvard and Yale must have seemed
very far away.

Here is Henri's description of the adjustments that he
made just to live in the New House:

*I had to come to terms with the fact that I had not lived a fami-
ly life since I was eighteen years old, and here I was faced with a large
house to be cleaned, big meals to be cooked, countless dishes to be
washed, and stacks of laundry to be done, not to mention shopping,
doctors' appointments, bookkeeping, transportation, and the never-end-
ing need for repairs. After thirty-seven years of living in schools where
all these things were taken care of, family life made me aware of my
lack of the most ordinary skills. Making a dinner for eleven people
filled me with great fear, and except for sunny-side-up eggs, every
request at breakfast, whether for pancakes, omelettes, French toast, or
waffles, threw me into confusion. Writing books and giving lectures
seemed like easy hills to climb compared to the mountainous complex-
ities of daily living. No wonder that I soon gave up on the idea that
some of us are handicapped and others not. [26]*

Learning from the Disabled

"Handicapped people have little, if anything, to show to the world. They have no degrees, no reputation, no influence, no connections with influential people. . . . They have to trust that they can receive and give pure love."

—The Road to Daybreak

Like many others who are called to live and work with people with disabilities, Henri's first feelings and attitudes toward the disabled were pity, concern, and a certain alarm at his own responsibility for the needs of people who were unable to care for themselves. However, as he became more involved with l'Arche, in France and then at Daybreak, he realized that l'Arche had a philosophy that was quite different from the world's way of thinking, as well as his own. One day he went apple picking and was struck that in l'Arche this outing became an opportunity to give to the handicapped a deeper sense of nature, of their own abilities, and of community support. Although he found himself thinking that he could have picked up the few apples they gathered in a matter of minutes, he was learning that there was more at stake at l'Arche than efficiency.

In fact, the disabled seemed to be living in the spirit that Jesus evoked in the Beatitudes and in his parables, in which the meek inherit the earth or a woman sweeps out her house in search of a single lost coin. In all these stories, overlooked and forgotten people and things end up being very important. Jesus also had much to say about God's care for children, sparrows, and "the lilies of the field, who do not toil or labor." The handicapped seemed to be living out this part of the gospel, giving and receiving love alone, not producing or serving or earning anything in the world's terms.

Although Nouwen was a master at simplifying huge theological topics, working with the disabled required a whole new approach from him. A great communicator, he was con-

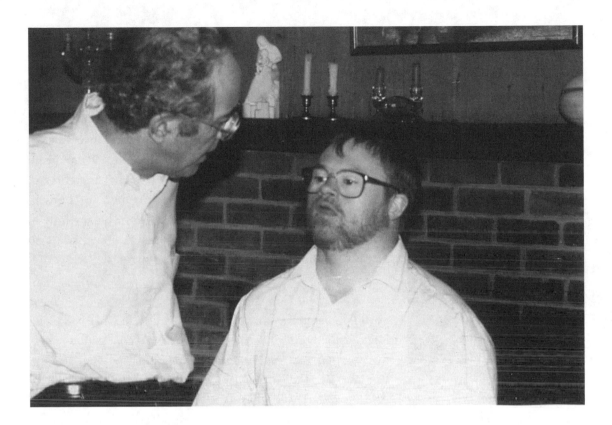

Henri in conversation with Gord Henry, a core member of L'Arche Daybreak. (Courtesy Henri Nouwen Literary Centre)

fronted with people who could not understand words. A man of action, he was confronted by people who could only move with difficulty. He had to learn a whole new way of reaching people. Ultimately it dawned on him that the disabled were teaching him and helping him as much or more than he was serving them. In their presence, the way he said Mass became very slow and meditative, and the presence of the disabled kept everyone's focus on the present moment. Henri learned to sweep away the theological abstractions that are part of the Mass, and make it clear that we are called to sit and eat with Jesus right now.

The life of humility and even the silence of those unable to speak became for Henri another witness to Christ. In their isolation, in their dependence on others, in their patience, and in the beauty of their simple thoughts and feelings, they

(Courtesy Henri Nouwen Literary Centre)

revealed to Henri new ways in which Christ was present in the world. "The kingdom belongs to such as these," as Jesus said. Here were people who did not read, cling to grudges, or hide their feelings. Those who were hurt showed their woundedness openly. Those who are happy broadcast their joy. By living with such openhearted people Henri and everyone at l'Arche were able to see how they might live lives more in keeping with the gospel of Jesus. The disabled members of l'Arche taught Henri simplicity. By loving him for himself, they taught him that he did not need to do or be anything in order to be accepted. Here is one of Henri's observations on living with the community:

> In one of our Daybreak houses lives Janice. She cannot speak and needs full-time care to live well. But she can walk, and she puts on the wall cutout hearts with the names of those for whom we want to pray. She does this with great enthusiasm and fervor every day of Lent. Thus she blesses all around the table in a special way.
>
> But there is more. All of us are not only little but also great. God has looked with mercy on our littleness and has made us sons and daughters of the Most High, people with the unique vocation to announce good news to the poor and liberate the captives. In our littleness we discover our wholeness; in our sickness we realize our joy; in the confession of our sin we come to see grace. Our littleness allows us to claim our greatness before God. [27]

"I started to see more clearly how Daybreak could help me not only to receive the little children, but also to become like one of them."

—The Road to Daybreak

Adam

Right from the outset of Henri's time at Daybreak he was asked to care for Adam by helping him do a morning routine. Adam was the most disabled member of the community. He and his brother Michael both lived at Daybreak. Adam began to have severe seizures at the age of three months that left him more vulnerable as time went on. He was unable to speak or walk without assistance; the only real activity he could carry out without help was eating with a spoon.

Henri Nouwen was at first quite unwilling to consider taking charge of dressing, bathing, and feeding Adam and then get-

"Adam was, like all of us, a limited person, more limited than most, and unable to express himself in words. But he was also a whole person and a blessed man. In his weakness he became a unique instrument of God's grace. He became a revelation of Christ among us."
—Adam

Adam Arnett. (Courtesy Photograph Series, Henri Nouwen Archives)

> *"Adam keeps revealing to me, over and over again and in his own clear way, that what makes us human is not primarily our minds but our hearts; it is not first of all our ability to think which gives us our particular identity in all of creation, but it is our ability to love."*
>
> —Finding My Way Home

ting him over to another building for his day program. Indeed, Henri had great difficulty making his own way safely through physical space; how could he take responsibility for someone else, particularly someone who could not speak and needed all sorts of attention? Weren't Adam and Henri particularly mismatched, since Henri was essentially a speaker, and Adam was someone who had never spoken a word in all his life?

The community leadership still insisted that Henri would benefit from getting to know Adam, despite his many fears and objections. So Henri began to help Adam, perhaps the most hands-on experience he had ever had in his life. The first attempts were awkward, and many times Henri was impatient and tried to rush through things, but as he became more comfortable with Adam, he did rather enjoy and take pride in his ability to do something so physical that involved another person.

He also began to discover Adam's special qualities. There was a peace that seemed to emanate from Adam, and Henri found himself able to talk to Adam about his plans and his problems. Although he could not be sure Adam understood him, their time together slowly became more fruitful and important. Just as some of the monks Henri had known lived in silence, Adam was a silent and peaceful presence that made itself felt. Slowly Henri began to see that Adam had a very real ministry to those around him, and that his patience and vulnerability were very Christian qualities. Christ said, "Blessed are the peacemakers," and Adam was a peacemaker of a very special sort.

One of the first things I was asked to do was to help Adam in the mornings. Adam is a twenty-five-year-old man. He does not speak. He cannot let you know if he likes his food or not, whether you are hurting him or not, whether he wants something or not. He seldom smiles. You are never sure if he recognizes you. For all the basic things of life—dressing and undressing, walking, eating, going to the bathroom—he needs careful attention. Every day he suffers from

Henri with Adam. (Courtesy Photograph Series, Henri Nouwen Archives)

"Each of us who has touched Adam has been made whole somewhere; it has been our common experience."
—Adam

epileptic seizures which often exhaust him so much that he needs hours of extra sleep to recuperate. In the beginning I was afraid to be with Adam. He is so fragile that I was always worried I would do something wrong. But gradually I came to know and love this stranger. As I gave him his bath, brushed his teeth, combed his hair, gave him his breakfast, and talked to him as if he could fully understand me, my fears were gradually cast out by emerging feelings of tenderness and care. I even began to miss him when I was away for a few days, and when home I came to enjoy just sitting with him, rubbing noses, caressing his face, or playing with his fingers. Thus a stranger became a friend. [28]

Sister Sue Mosteller

T hus it was that Henri Nouwen found a home at
Daybreak, and at Daybreak he also found a family.
Every day was filled with people, just like before, but
the pace was slower and the gravitational pull of the community strong and comforting. As the years passed he was able to
slow down somewhat and appreciate the small miracles and
simple people whom he had been called to care for. He never
became a quiet person, but after several years of being part of
l'Arche he was no longer the one-man whirlwind of activity
and outreach that he had been during his university years.

At Daybreak Henri Nouwen was able to examine and
work on his craving for intimacy and interaction. The l'Arche
community has the resources to offer support to members who
need it, and at Daybreak Henri received some of the attention
and support he sought for so long. The community leaders
reminded him not to overextend himself. They reminded him
that now he had a home, and he needed to spend time there
with his family. When he traveled, very often one of the core
members went with him. The community made sure that
Henri was not allowed to get too busy and become his own
worst enemy, something he was quite capable of doing.

Someone who is not mentioned very often but who
played an enormous role in his life at this time is Sue Mosteller,
a sister of Saint Joseph. There were and are many wonderful
people at Daybreak and Henri loved them all, but Sue
Mosteller was special. She was special because of her background and training as a celibate religious, just like Henri himself, and because of her great common sense and competence.

Opposite: *Henri with Sister Sue
Mosteller in a play staged at the
Winter Garden Theater in Toronto
to celebrate the twenty-fifth
anniversary of L'Arche Daybreak,
January 1995.* (Photo by Doug Wiebe.
Courtesy Henri Nouwen Literary Centre)

(Courtesy Photograph Series, Henri Nouwen
Archives)

When Henri needed to be reminded or confronted or asked
to do things differently, it often fell to Sister Sue to be the messenger. Although they had a common background as Roman
Catholics and celibate religious, there were many ways in
which these two people were not at all alike. If Henri could be
emotional and crazy on occasion, Sister Sue was level-headed
and careful. There were numerous confrontations between
them, but over the years these two leaders of the Daybreak
community learned from each other and grew together. If Jean
Vanier was Henri's older brother in Christ, then Sue Mosteller
was to Henri a true sister in the Lord.

Henri Nouwen had many close friends, more than anyone
has a right to have, but of all these friends it was Sue Mosteller
who was entrusted, after his death, with managing his affairs
and shaping his legacy. During his last sabbatical, she had taken
his place as the community's pastor. Competent and caring, she
was a unique person in Henri Nouwen's later years, the one
who most challenged and complemented Henri during his life
and the one who took up his work when he was gone.

Plunging into Crisis

enri Nouwen had gone to l'Arche not only to minister to others but to heal his own soul. He was looking for a home and also for a way to ease the pain he felt inside. Because he was such an inspiring and wonderful teacher, it is easy to forget that Henri Nouwen's own woundedness dogged his steps throughout his life. He suffered from a strong sense of shame and a longing for love and intimacy that held him firmly in their grip. The family atmosphere at l'Arche was a balm for his wounds. Certainly he received much healing in his first, formative years at l'Arche, but then the turbulent darkness that lay beneath many of Henri's remarks and insights surfaced stronger than ever. The breakdown of an important friendship was at the heart of the crisis that at one point threatened to destroy him.

Nathan Ball, who had become Daybreak community's leader, was this close friend. When they first met in Trosly, Henri was fifty-five and Nathan was only twenty-eight, but they were both men of heart who wanted to follow God and who were searching for his will. Like many heartfelt Christians before them, they discovered in the other person one of the wonderful mysteries of our tradition: spiritual friendship. The spiritual friend is someone who so complements our spiritual journey that we find God in a new way through that person, either through their encouragement, their sympathy, or sometimes even through their opposition to our plans and purposes. In such powerful relationships, our way to God seems to go straight through that person.

Henri became very attached to Nathan, even when they

"I was going through the deep human struggle to believe in my belovedness even when I had nothing to be proud of. . . . Yes, I was considered a good, even a noble person because I was helping the poor! But now that the last crutch had been taken away, I was challenged to believe that even when I had nothing to show for myself, I was still God's beloved son."

—Adam

(Photo by Mary Carney, used with permissiom)

were in France. He was delighted that Nathan also was headed for Toronto when he decided to go there, and Nathan's rise to leadership in the Daybreak community was a joy for Henri. He felt that Nathan understood him, that he could tell him anything, and, ultimately, that Nathan loved him, and Nathan did. However, living in community also forced Henri to confront his dependence on Nathan and the way that, as he later wrote, Nathan had become the "center of my emotional stability."[29] Henri could be too demanding of friends and family, and Nathan came to the point of feeling overwhelmed by the crucial role that he had come to play in Henri's life.

When Henri realized that Nathan was unable to share so much with him and was withdrawing from Henri, he was first devastated, then began to spiral into a complete depression. Henri felt abandoned, was inconsolably shattered, and became paralyzed with an overwhelming sense of his own worthlessness. His anguish grew to the point that he could not function, and he withdrew from the community to a shelter for persons undergoing spiritual emergencies in distant Winnipeg. There he remained for six months. In Winnipeg he underwent a deep and intensive therapy in the care of a two person spiritual emergency team composed of a man and a woman. They visited him every day and together they explored the darkness and pain that Nathan's need for distance had exposed. It was Henri Nouwen's darkest hour, and he often felt that he would never emerge from that darkness and never again return to l'Arche or to ministry anywhere.

Yet he did heal, and he did return. Even his relationship with Nathan was ultimately restored, and this time on a healthier basis. Henri realized that he could only find all that he hoped Nathan might provide within himself and within the embrace of God, but there was a long journey which he made before arriving at this knowledge.

Many years later the world learned of Henri's profound crisis because, through it all, he had kept a secret journal, not

Cover of The Inner Voice of Love *(Doubleday, 1996), reflections written during Nouwen's time of crisis.*

"You have been wounded in many ways. The more you open yourself to being healed, the more you will discover how deep your wounds are. . . . The great challenge is living your wounds through instead of thinking them through. . . . Your heart is greater than your wounds."
—The Inner Voice of Love

With Nathan Ball at a Daybreak picnic, 1991. (Courtesy Photograph Series, Henri Nouwen Archives)

intended for publication. This private journal was written in the form of admonitions to himself. Yet sharing his journal with others had been a positive experience, and this led him to publish, eight years later, even this secret journal. Called *The Inner Voice of Love,* this is Nouwen's most intimate and penetrating work, one in which Henri, the wounded healer, speaks to Henri, the wounded person:

> *What is your pain? It is the experience of not receiving what you most need. It is a place of emptiness where you feel sharply the absence of the love you most desire. To go back to that place is hard, because you are confronted there with your wounds as well as with your powerlessness to heal yourself. You are so afraid of that place that you think of it as a place of death. Your instinct for survival makes you run away and go looking for something else that can give you a sense of at-home-ness, even though you know full well that it can't be found out in the world. You have to begin to trust that your experience of emptiness is not the final experience, that beyond it is a place where you are being held in love.*[30]

Celebrating Life

One of the special attributes of l'Arche community, one which amounts to an "antidote to civilization," is its dedication to celebration. True to its French origins, the l'Arche community knows the importance of sharing meals and making eating special. At l'Arche no one's birthday passes unnoticed, and all special occasions are likewise celebrated—Paolo is back from Brazil, let's celebrate! Today is Antoine's birthday, let's get together! Let us have a special meal, because Denise is leaving, or because Advent has begun, or because we have had a great week!

Celebration is a l'Arche priority for an important reason:

"It is the presence of Jesus among us, real and concrete, that gives us hope. It is eating and drinking here that creates the desire for the heavenly banquet. . . . Who better than severely mentally handicapped people can teach us this liberating truth? . . . They do not dwell upon the future. Instead they say, 'Feed me, dress me, touch me, hold me. . . . Kiss me, speak to me. It is good to be here together now.'"
—Lifesigns

First communion for Janet Whitney Brown. (Courtesy Photograph Series, Henri Nouwen Archives)

Above left: *Henri playing the drums.* (Photo by Paula Kilcoyne. Courtesy Henri Nouwen Literary Centre).

Above right: *Henri being "born again" as a clown on his sixtieth birthday in 1992.* (Courtesy Photograph Series, Henri Nouwen Archives)

"For anyone who has the courage to enter our human sorrows deeply, there is a revelation of joy, hidden like a precious stone in the wall of a dark cave."

—Can You Drink the Cup?

L'Arche, as its name implies, is a refuge from a world that can be uncaring and is often inhuman, a world that glorifies and celebrates the glamorous and successful few and depersonalizes many of the rest. By taking the time and the trouble to honor everyone in the community, l'Arche heals and restores people who have internalized the world's disdain. Sharing meals and celebrating is also part of the glue that holds any family or community together, so celebration is rightly at the heart of the l'Arche community.

Henri was very moved by the l'Arche experience of celebration, and he found particularly remarkable the importance of creating what l'Arche calls a "life story book." A life story book is a book that l'Arche members create to tell the story of their lives. It can be a scrapbook or a memoir or anything in between. It contains photos, letters, and reminiscences. The message of the life book is that every person has a story, every life is important, and every life should be shared and celebrated. In one of his books[31] Henri tells the story of Bill, who arrived in the community after a very troubled childhood, a childhood he chose to forget. He rebuilt his life at Daybreak, and even began to acknowledge the pain of his early years. For Bill, creating a life story book was the final step in his journey towards self-knowledge and self-esteem. Bill often accompanied Henri on his trips outside Daybreak, and he took his life story book on these trips and shared it with everyone who showed any interest. Bill had become someone who believed his life meant something for himself and for others.

Birthdays need to be celebrated. I think it is more important to celebrate a birthday than a successful exam, a promotion or a victory. Because to celebrate a birthday means to say to someone: "Thank you for being you." Celebrating a birthday is exalting life and being glad for it. On a birthday we do not say: "Thanks for what you did, or said, or accomplished." No, we say: "Thank you for being born and being among us." On birthdays we celebrate the present. We do not complain about what happened or speculate about what will happen, but we lift someone up and let everyone say: "We love you."[32]

Above: (Photo by Frank Hamilton, used with permission)

Left: *Henri with Bill van Buren.* (Courtesy Henri Nouwen Literary Centre)

Flying High

One of the biggest adventures of Henri Nouwen's later years began in Germany. He was there to visit a publisher, and during the visit he was invited to go along to see a circus performance. Nouwen had always identified with clowns, and had even suggested in his book, *Clowning in Rome*, that being a spiritual person, especially a celibate or a contemplative, was in fact a lot like being a clown. There in the circus in Germany were the clowns he loved, but it was another act that riveted his attention: the trapeze performance. The trapeze was the glittering highlight of everything under the big top. The sight of people flying through the air in graceful arcs and tumbles was inspiring, but even more so the fact that it was all about community. The trapeze artists were clearly only able to fly by working together.

Henri Nouwen succumbed to an instant obsessive fascination that day in Germany, the first time he saw the Flying Rodleighs, as the South African trapeze troupe was called. He returned for the next performance, and the next. He asked if he might meet the troupe and then wanted to see them and talk to them again and again. He was so taken with everything that the Rodleighs were doing that he arranged later to follow their act from city to city and live in a trailer like they did.

What was so compelling about the trapeze? Here Henri thought he had encountered another, and perhaps the perfect metaphor for the spiritual life. First there is risk, the leap into the air, then the spectacular flight, and then the return to safety as the flyer landed in the grip of the catcher. He learned about the training, preparation, and discipline behind each maneuver,

Opposite above: *The Flying Rodleighs in mid-air.* (Photo by Ron van den Bosch, used with permission)

Below: *Henri attempting a flight on the trapeze.* (Photo by Ron van den Bosch, used with permission)

> *"When I first saw the Rodleighs, something very deep and intimate within me was touched. They brought back in a vivid way the longings I had had as a seventeen-year-old boy for communion, community, and intimacy. . . . There in the air I saw the artistic realization of my deepest yearnings."*
> —Sabbatical Journey

Henri with his circus friends.
(Photo by Ron van den Bosch. Courtesy
Henri Nouwen Literary Centre)

and how the troupe dealt with flaws and failure. He found out
that acrobatics were so intense and immediate that when the
Rodleighs were up in the air they could not dwell on anything
but the moves they were performing. They put aside anger, sorrow, and jealousy. In its own way, the trapeze was purifying.

The circus became like a new horizon opening up for
Henri Nouwen. If Yale and Harvard were journeys of the
mind, and l'Arche a journey of the heart, then the trapeze was
all about the body, and Henri felt that he himself could and
should fly if he was ever going to understand it. Thus one day
Henri himself climbed up to the platform, connected his har-
ness to the safety lines, and made his own maiden voyage on

the trapeze. He was exhilarated and elated at the feeling, and had to do it again and again. He said it was the most exciting experience of his life.

It was Henri's plan to write a book about the trapeze and about the Rodleighs—a special book, different from all his other ones. He never wrote that special book, but he did do a very engaging short film on the trapeze, called *Angels Over the Net*. The one most vivid insight of that film is that a flyer cannot fly without trusting himself to the catcher. To the casual observer, the catcher may be almost an unseen figure alongside the glorious flyer, but within the troupe, it is the catcher who is the real star. In our lives we also have to trust an unseen, but equally important figure: God. As we take our risks and make our own plunges and rolls, we do so in the knowledge that God is there, like the catcher, to receive us and carry us home.

"Living in a community with very wounded people, I came to see that I had lived most of my life as a tightrope artist trying to walk on a high, thin cable from one tower to the other, always waiting for the applause when I had not fallen off and broken my leg."
—In the Name of Jesus

Talking with a member of the Flying Rodleighs. (Photo by Ron van den Bosch, used with permission)

The Return of the Prodigal Son

"For hours I looked at the splendid drawings and paintings [Rembrandt] created in the midst of all his setbacks, disillusionments and grief, and I came to understand how from his brush there emerged the figure of a nearly blind man holding his son in a gesture of all-forgiving compassion. One must have died many deaths and cried many tears to have painted a portrait of God in such humility."

—The Return of the
Prodigal Son

There have been few spiritual teachers as interested in art as was Henri Nouwen. Vincent van Gogh was like a soul mate to him, and he also studied the work of Marc Chagall. However, the greatest insight and the finest book he ever wrote were triggered by a work by neither of these artists, but by Rembrandt. The painting by the Dutch master that changed Nouwen's life was *The Return of the Prodigal Son*. This canvas pictures a scene from one of the more dramatic parables of Jesus: in the story a man has two sons, one loyal and obedient, the other a goof-off and a failure. This directionless son demands his inheritance from his father and departs to seek his fortune. His father's money is soon wasted away and the son is reduced to the unclean occupation of keeping pigs. He is hungry, wretched, and ruined. When he sinks to the level of envying the pigs their miserable fodder, he comes to his senses and humbly returns to his father's house. Against all odds, the father receives him home, not with censure, but with a lavish party.

Rembrandt's painting portrays the moment when the story reaches a climax: the prodigal kneels before his father. The father figure is bearded and distinctly Jewish in appearance. He wears an enormous red cloak, which stands out warmly against the dark background. Kneeling before him is a prodigal, dressed in a yellow tunic. His head is shaved and bowed into the shadow of his father's embrace.

When Nouwen saw a poster of this picture for the first time in Trosly, he says that his heart leapt inside him. He immediately identified with that son, kneeling and vulnerable—ever looking for shelter and acceptance. The image remained in his

heart. Two years later he had an opportunity to see the actual painting. Henri was invited to go to Russia by his American friends, Bob Massie and Dana Robert. One reason he accepted the offer to travel was because he thought he would be able to visit the Hermitage in Saint Petersburg, where Rembrandt's painting is found. When he arrived at the museum and then was escorted to the hall where *The Return of the Prodigal Son* hangs, he felt shocked and overwhelmed. It was only when he saw Rembrandt's work before him that he realized that the poster he had been meditating on for two years was only a detail of a larger canvas that included other figures: there to the side was the older brother, and other friends of the household were in the background. Henri spent days meditating before the picture and taking notes. From that experience came what many regard as his finest book, also called *The Return of the Prodigal Son*. It is subtitled *A Meditation on Fathers, Brothers, and Sons*.

From the first, Nouwen saw himself as someone like the prodigal. His relationship with his own father had often been strained and marked by Henri's need for a level of approval and

Henri with his father, Laurent Nouwen, Geysteren, 1993. (Courtesy Henri Nouwen Literary Centre)

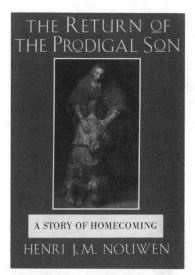

Cover of The Return of the
Prodigal Son *(Doubleday, 1992).*

*"When I first saw
Rembrandt's Prodigal
Son, I could never have
dreamt that becoming the
repentant son was only a
step on the way to becom-
ing the welcoming father.
I now see that the hands
that forgive, console, heal,
and offer a festive meal
must become my own."*

—The Return of the
Prodigal Son

intimacy that was hard for his father to understand. With this book, in some ways, he renews this old quest for his father's love; in fact, the book is dedicated to his father on the occasion of his ninetieth birthday.

Henri's identification with the prodigal son was immediate, but as he continued to discuss the painting and his feelings with friends, someone pointed out to him that he ought to also see the parallels between himself and the older brother—the dutiful figure so prone to resentment. He accepted this insight, and it added another dimension to the painting. As he extended his meditation even further, the kneeling son became a figure of Christ returning to God the Father. His own sense of identification also continued to shift, moving through the elder brother to finally rest on the father. Becoming the father is becoming the one who reconciles and welcomes; to "be the father" was for Nouwen to finally understand Rembrandt's painting and the way of Christian maturity and service.

More than a meditation, Nouwen's *The Return of the Prodigal Son* is a spiritual vision. It is a book about forgiveness, thankfulness, and the mystery of family and of self and of God. Asked to name one book to recommend to others, Hillary Clinton chose this Nouwen book, which had helped her through her darkest hours in the White House.

As the Father, I have to believe that all the human heart desires can be found at home. As the Father, I have to be free from the need to wander around curiously and to catch up with what I might otherwise perceive as missed childhood opportunities. As the Father, I have to know that, indeed, my youth is over and that playing youthful games is nothing but a ridiculous attempt to cover up the truth that I am old and close to death. As the Father, I have to dare to carry the responsibility of a spiritually adult person and dare to trust that the real joy and real fulfillment can only come from welcoming home those who have been hurt and wounded on their life's journey, and loving them with a love that neither asks nor expects anything in return. [33]

New York, New York

Yale University in New Haven, Connecticut, is not at all far from New York, one of the greatest cities of the world. Indeed, all of Connecticut is very much in the New York orbit. Henri had first seen America aboard an ocean liner entering the New York harbor, and the city had always beckoned to him. New York was also home to some of Henri's favorite people. The most unlikely of these was Fred Bratman. Fred met Henri at Yale. He had gone there to interview Henri for an article to appear in the *New York Times*. That interview did not proceed very far before Henri had turned the tables on the young reporter and started to interview him and query him about his hopes and dreams.

(Photo by Robert Quast/Philadelphia Support/The Netherlands)

Fred admitted he was frustrated. He wanted to write a novel, not be a reporter, but he needed money to live. Nouwen responded to this story in his typically amazing way by inviting Fred to drop everything and come up to Yale. Henri would find the money, and Fred would write his book. Fred was at first distrustful of Henri, wondering what this man really wanted. Fred was Jewish, and somewhat secular and cynical; in many ways he was the typical New Yorker. Why was Henri so interested in helping him?

In the end Fred did accept Nouwen's offer, and thus began a very interesting friendship between two people who did not have much in common. Fred and Henri stayed in touch after Fred returned to New York. On his many visits there Henri would visit Fred and marvel at the decidedly different life he was leading. It was urban and fast-paced, almost jet-propelled. It was a Jewish lifestyle, but Fred's Judaism was not observant. Being with Fred taught Henri how to think outside his Christian box, even outside his "spiritual" box. Fred was a truly secular person.

Another important New York friendship was with Wendy

and Jay Greer. The Greers were an Episcopal couple with a Park Avenue apartment and a generous spirit like that of Henri himself. Their deep friendship began when Wendy, who had read and studied Henri's books for fifteen years, wrote him a long letter, indeed, one with a page for each of those fifteen years. They began to correspond, then met, and Henri began to visit the Greers; ultimately, they became very close friends. The Greers found Henri fascinating, and he appreciated the love and energy of these accomplished people. It was actually through that firm friendship that much of Henri's ministry to others was given a permanent form after his death, when Wendy created the U.S. Henri Nouwen Society. She also gathered his writings on prayer into a volume called *The Only Necessary Thing*. Wendy Greer has played a crucial role in keeping the Nouwen legacy vibrant and on track.

For Henri Nouwen, New York, that lively city, became another place that he could feel welcome and appreciated. He loved the city and he loved his friends who lived there, and, in turn, they loved him, too.

I vividly remember when I arrived for the first time in New York. . . . I can still recall the feeling I had when at 7:00 in the morning we passed the Statue of Liberty and approached the imposing skyline of Manhattan Island. . . . Now, thirty-four years later, I have come to know New York, its beauty and its ugliness, its wealth and its poverty, its open parks and little alleys, its splendor and its squalor. But I am not longer a tourist here. . . . I came to know New Yorkers, people who had lived in New York all their lives, worked there, went to church there, and had their circles of friends there. Gradually New York City became smaller, friendlier, more intimate, and much safer for me. Tonight I am just full of gratitude for being invited into this city by good friends, Wendy and Jay, and by other loving and generous people. Through them and many others, the United States has become my country. And although I have my home in Canada, I still feel very much at home in this country and especially in this city.[34]

Confronting Death and Dying

"Years after my mother's death, she continues to bear fruit in my life. I am deeply aware that many of my major decisions since her death have been guided by the Spirit of Jesus, which she continues to send me."

—Our Greatest Gift

Henri Nouwen never dealt with issues in the abstract. If something did not impact him or those near him personally, he was not interested in writing or speaking about it. Of course, Henri could surprise and even mildly shock some of his writers by exploring openly experiences and feelings that most consider private and personal; this was part of his decision to "lay down his life for others."[35] Sometimes this meant revealing hard experiences that most people keep to themselves. Publishing *The Inner Voice of Love* was one example of this surprising openness.

Henri with his mother during her last visit at Yale. (Nouwen family albums)

Another example can be found at a much earlier point in his life. During Henri's time at Yale University he suffered a great loss. His parents visited him from Holland, and on that visit his mother became gravely ill. Returning to Holland, she was operated on and diagnosed with cancer. She only lived a few more days. Henri rushed to Holland and was with his mother as she faced death surrounded by the family. Losing his mother, who was also his confidante and emotional mainstay, was a terrible blow for Henri. He could only process the experience by writing it down, and his reflections became a small book, *In Memoriam,* which rather bravely details the pain and confusion his mother experienced and his family's reaction to her loss. This was followed by publication of a letter he wrote six months later to his father, entitled *A Letter of Consolation.* There he tells his father, "Ever since we saw her face still in the hospital, we have wondered what death really is. It is a question mother has left us with, and we want to face it, enter it, explore it, and let it grow in us."[36]

In both these books Henri takes a very troubling experience from his own life, his mother's death, and brings out the redemptive and faith dimension of what had happened. He does not hesitate to record his real feelings or the details of the experience, which he puts down almost as a painter would arrange figures and objects in a death-scene tableau.

This was also the beginning of an exploration of the theme of death and dying that would be a constant throughout his life. In his later years there would be two more serious books about death, and again, they were very personal; the death Henri was confronting in these books was his own. One of these books was *Our Greatest Gift,* a short work that Henri wrote while on a writing retreat in Germany. In it, Henri claims dying as something that we can own and embrace, just as we might our own life. In *Our Greatest Gift,* Henri explores some of his recent experiences of death and confronts his own mortality and hopes and fears, but he finds that death is not

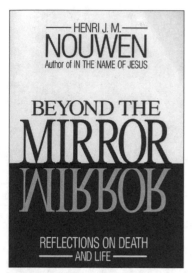

Cover of Beyond the Mirror
(Crossroad, 1990).

"*I wonder more and more whether I am not given some extra years so that I can live them from the other side. . . . Perhaps I am given an opportunity to live more theologically and to help others to do the same without their having to be hit by the mirror of a passing van.*"

—Beyond the Mirror

foreign or unwelcome. Dying is something that we do, and can even do well.

The other book, *Beyond the Mirror*, is a rather remarkable recounting of a near-death experience. While at Daybreak Henri had foolishly ventured out on an icy morning to walk to Richmond Hill to prepare His-Fu, a blind and severely handicapped core member, for his day. As he walked along the road, out of sorts with the world but determined to succeed in his purpose, he was struck by the mirror of a passing van. The resulting internal injuries were severe, and Henri was operated on, leaving him close to death.

As he drifted in and out of consciousness and found himself standing on the portal of the next world, he felt a readiness to leave this life and experience what lay beyond.

He writes:

What I experienced then was something I had never experienced before: pure and unconditional love. Better still, what I experienced was an intensely personal presence, a presence that pushed all my fears aside and said, "Come, don't be afraid. I love you." A very gentle, non-judgmental presence: a presence that simply asked me to trust and trust completely. I hesitate to speak simply about Jesus, because of my concern that the name of Jesus might not evoke the full divine presence that I experienced. It was not a warm light, a rainbow, or an open door that I saw, but a human yet divine presence that I felt, inviting me to come closer and to let go of all fears.[37]

Henri Nouwen, to his own great disappointment, did not die. He felt that he clung to life out of a sense of unresolved issues and conflicts. He also felt that God had denied him entry into the next world. He found he needed to settle in his own mind the question of why he had not died as he had wished, but he realized how much resolution the experience had granted him. He saw life in greater perspective, and, as he would try to do more deliberately in *Our Greatest Gift*, he

Henri with his sister Laurien, his father, and his brother Paul at his mother's grave. (Courtesy Henri Nouwen Literary Centre)

befriended death. In the depths of this experience he had found Christ not only present, but showering him with love. He could not help but feel the irony that his friends rejoiced in his recovery, while he was left feeling ambivalent about returning to a world that is not as close to Jesus as he had been while standing on the edge of eternity.

Thus, for Henri Nouwen, death held more promise than fear. Death was an entryway into the next stage in our journey, and, for him, death was also the resolution of a lifetime of wondering and waiting to see God. He did not approach death dogmatically, yet he faced it with great certainty that death is a return, a reentry, into the blessed presence of God. Grief he explored and grasped and also befriended, but any grief over the death of friends and relations was swallowed up, finally, in the promise of God's welcome into a higher reality quite free of the distractions and darkness that are part of our life in this world. Being near death, he had found he was near to God:

> *I have lost much of the peace and freedom that was given to me in the hospital. I regret it; I even grieve over it. Once again there are many people, many projects, many pulls. Never enough time and space to do it all and feel totally satisfied. I am no longer as centered and focused as I was during my illness. I wish I were.*[38]

> *"The real question before our death, then, is not How much can I still accomplish, or How much influence can I still exert? But, How can I live so that I can continue to be fruitful when I am no longer here among my family and friends?"*
> —Our Greatest Gift

The Life of the Beloved

Cover of *Life of the Beloved*
(Crossroad, 1992).

In the last years of Henri Nouwen's life there emerged in his writing a powerful theme, a new idea, which might count as his greatest contribution to the teachings of Christianity. It was an idea many years in the making, and it had to do with Jesus. Henri encountered Jesus in the Eucharist more than he did anywhere else in life, and as he meditated on how Jesus took bread, blessed it, broke it, and gave it to others, he realized that Jesus was similarly taken, blessed by God at his baptism, broken on the cross, and then given to the world. The Eucharistic ritual of the breaking and distribution of the bread mirrored Christ's life. As he took this idea further, he realized that every believer also is "taken, blessed, broken, and given." Each one of us becomes just like the bread that Jesus had held.

In Henri's estimation, everyone who believes is first "chosen" by God, and placed in their unique circumstances in life, then "blessed," in the same way that Christ was blessed in his baptism. A blessing is pure affirmation, and it empowers us. The blessing of God reveals to us our true nature as daughters and sons of God. This was what happened in the life of Jesus: he was blessed by God the Father during his baptism. Like Jesus, we are also "broken" by life's sorrows. However, the result of our being broken is that, again like Jesus, we are "given" to the world. Our lives are a gift.

In developing this beautiful meditation—taken, blessed, broken, and given—Henri began to realize that the life of Jesus and the life of his followers had many other parallels. He took this thought further when he wrote his great book, *The Return of the Prodigal Son.* There he explored more deeply the critical

(Photo by Peter Weiskel, used with permission)

experience of Jesus during his baptism, and the blessing that he had received from his father. As a believer, Henri felt that that same blessing, "You are my beloved Son, in whom I am well pleased," was his to claim as well. Henri, and all of us, must begin to believe that we are the Beloved of God, that as "heirs to the promise" we share in the blessing of Jesus.

This is a huge statement, considering how little any sane person identifies with Jesus, yet in another book published the same year Henri pressed his point further. He wrote *Life of the Beloved* at the invitation of Fred Bratman. It was intended to be a spiritual book for Fred and his friends, people who had little connection to Jesus, but in the end, it, too, is a book about Jesus and how Jesus relates to them. In this book Henri extends the mantle of blessing, and the words, "You are my Beloved," to the Fred Bratmans of this world. Everyone, he explains, is on the same path as Jesus: taken, blessed, broken, and given. It is a universal paradigm that ties everyone into Jesus and into God.

Life of the Beloved is thus the most universal of Nouwen's many books. Here he extends to everyone his vision—a vision

"The greatest gift my friendship can give to you is the gift of your Belovedness. I can give that gift only insofar as I have claimed it for myself. Isn't that what friendship is all about: giving to each other the gift of our Belovedness?"

—Life of the Beloved

(Courtesy Photograph Series, Henri Nouwen Archives)

of every person standing under God's blessing and fatherly embrace, of every person coming to stand next to Christ not by some moral effort but by virtue of God's love. How can one come to the Father by any other path than that of Jesus?

The unfathomable mystery of God is that God is a lover who wants to be loved. The one who created us is waiting for our response to the love that gave us our being. God not only says: "You are my Beloved." God also asks: "Do you love me?" and offers us countless chances to say "Yes." That is the spiritual life: the chance to say "Yes" to our inner truth. The spiritual life, thus understood, radically changes everything. Being born and growing up, leaving home and finding a career, being praised and being rejected, walking and resting, praying and playing, becoming ill and being healed—yes, living and dying— they all become expressions of that divine question: "Do you love me?" And at every point of the journey there is a chance to say "Yes" and the choice to say "No."[39]

Can You Drink the Cup?

The Eucharist was at the core of Henri Nouwen's life. As a priest he celebrated the Eucharist every day, and his daily meditations on the last meal of Jesus with his disciples yielded some very deep realizations. One day he found himself pausing over the words of Jesus, "Can you drink the cup I will drink?" and suddenly understanding the profundity of its implications. This realization led to the last book he saw published in his lifetime, entitled *Can You Drink the Cup?* This book is a deep but also simple reflection of how much the Eucharist gathers up and reflects our lives.

In contrast to the tendency of traditional Catholicism to see the Eucharist primarily as a holy manifestation of Christ among us, Nouwen teaches that the Eucharist embodies a very human and very simple gesture, a moment of fellowship and understanding that we share with Jesus. He reminds us that eating and drinking together at a table is a very important expression of who we are and how we live. Every day we show hospitality and deepen our friendships by eating and drinking with others. Around the table we learn and celebrate our family's traditions, toast our successes, mourn our losses, and seek reconciliation. Table fellowship is a sign of intimacy and, in a very real sense, a place where we examine our life and find its meaning. The table of Jesus needs to become again what it once was, a summing up and a sharing of all the toils, experiences, and aspirations of all those who are made one by the sharing of Christ's body and blood.

In *Can You Drink the Cup?* Henri reflects quite a bit about his own life, and how he grew up in a family and around a table.

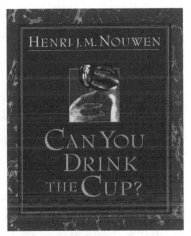

Cover of Can You Drink the Cup? *(Ave Maria, 1996).*

He makes it clear that the Eucharist is about bringing our lives into communion with others and with God. There is for Nouwen a seamless continuity between our lives and the lives of God, and the greatest point of connection is at the table.

I still remember a family dinner long ago in the Netherlands. It was a special occasion, but I have forgotten whether it was a birthday, a wedding, or an anniversary. Since I was still a young boy, I was not allowed to drink wine, but I was fascinated by the way the grown-ups were drinking their wine! After the wine had been poured into the glasses, my uncle took his glass, put both of his hands around the cup,

"Every time we invite Jesus into our homes, that is to say, into our life with all its light and dark sides, and offer him the place of honor at our table, he takes the bread and the cup and hands them to us saying: 'Take and eat, this is my body. Take and drink, this is my blood. Do this to remember me.'"

—With Burning Hearts

(Photo by Mary Carney, used with permission)

"When we lift the cup of our life and share with one another our sufferings and joys in mutual vulnerability, the new covenant can become visible among us. The surprise of it all is that it is often the least among us who reveal to us that our cup is a cup of blessings."
—Can You Drink the Cup?

(Courtesy Photograph Series, Henri Nouwen Archives)

moved the glass gently while letting the aroma enter his nostrils, looked at all the people around the table, lifted it up, took a little sip, and said: "Very good . . . a very good wine . . . let me see the bottle . . . it must be a fiftier."

This was my uncle Anton, my mother's oldest brother, priest, monsignor, authority on many things, good wines being one of them. Every time uncle Anton came to family dinners, he had a comment to make about the wine that was served. . . . One thing I learned from it all: drinking wine is more than just drinking. You have to know what you are drinking, and you have to be able to talk about it. Similarly, just living life is not enough. We must know what we are living. A life that is not reflected upon isn't worth living. It belongs to the essence of being human that we contemplate our life, think about it, discuss it, evaluate it, and form opinions about it. . . . Holding the cup of life means looking critically at what we are living. . . . When we drink the cup without holding it first, we may simply get drunk and wander around aimlessly.[40]

A Final Sabbatical

"I feel strange! Very happy and very scared at the same time. I have always dreamt about a whole year without appointments, meetings, lectures, travels, letters, and phone calls, a year completely open to let something radically new happen. But can I do it? Can I let go of all the things that make me feel useful and significant?"

—Sabbatical Journey

During most of Henri Nouwen's last year he was on sabbatical and staying with friends in the United States or Europe. He seemed to these friends to be somewhat exhausted and indeed very much in need of a rest. However, Henri Nouwen, even in his mature years, was not very good at resting. He was always busy talking or writing or phoning someone or arranging a meeting. Indeed, by the end of his sabbatical he had become quite caught up in creating community wherever he found himself and in ministering to those who arrived to see him. He could be maddeningly contradictory in this regard—going off somewhere new to be alone and then inviting everyone to come and visit him!

The time away from Daybreak was still a fruitful one for Henri. Many important insights began to take shape during

(Photo by Robert Jonas, used with permission)

With Rachel and Megan Christensen in Madison, New Jersey, July 1996 (two months before Nouwen's death). (Photo by Michael Christensen)

this working sabbatical. Perhaps the most important of these concerned his disabled friend, Adam Arnett. While Henri was staying with his friend Peggy McDonald in New Jersey he received word that Adam was mortally ill. Hearing that his friend was dying, Henri immediately rushed back to Toronto and was present there with the Daybreak community and with Adam's family when he passed away. He took part in Adam's funeral, and, as he stood over the coffin, among many other thoughts that went through his mind, he realized that Adam was only thirty-three years old, the same age Jesus had been at his death.

Somehow that thought and the reflections on the scope of Adam's life after he died began to fuse together with Henri's powerful meditation on ordinary people sharing in Christ's blessing. During much of his sabbatical Henri had been thinking about being like Jesus and taking the example of Jesus more seriously. He knew that most people could never imagine their lives having any correlation with the life of Jesus, but he thought that this was due to few people understanding how

(Courtesy Henri Nouwen Literary Centre)

much God loved them. Suddenly he realized what it was that he needed to say: he set aside the manuscript he had begun to write on the Apostle's Creed, and he started to compose the book that would be published after his death as *Adam: God's Beloved*. Henri did not live to put this book in final form. It was edited after his death by Sr. Sue Mosteller.

There was much that Henri wanted to say about Adam. In the first place, Adam had been a special person, someone who in his silence and vulnerability still was able to project a profound sense of peace. There was something so spiritual about Adam that many people benefited from spending time with him. But his book is not just a eulogy. In *Adam: God's Beloved*, Henri sets out to tell the story of Adam's life, and he does this in a provocative way, by setting it within the traditional framework of the life of Christ: hidden years, desert, public life, passion, death, burial, and resurrection. Moving back and forth between the very limited and helpless life that Adam lived and

In California during his sabbatical, 1996. (Courtesy Photograph Series, Henri Nouwen Archives)

(Photo by Frank Hamilton, used with permission)

"What to do with this inner wound that is so easily touched and starts bleeding again? It is such a familiar wound. It has been with me for many years. I don't think this wound—this immense need for affection, and this immense fear of rejection—will ever go away. It is there to stay, but maybe for a good reason. Perhaps it is a gateway to my salvation, a door to glory, and a passage to freedom!"

—Sabbatical Journey

comparisons to the life of Christ, Henri makes a very bold statement. Adam's life had dignity, purpose, and importance. Adam had a ministry, just like Jesus. People had been blessed in many ways by Adam's Christ-like example, despite his obvious limitations.

The message behind *Adam: God's Beloved* is that not only are all of us God's Beloved, but that the life of Jesus can be our life, too. By showing the parallels between the life of a very dis-

Adam

God's Beloved

Cover of Adam: God's Beloved
(Orbis, 1997).

abled person like Adam and Jesus Christ, Henri collapses the enormous distance between Jesus and all of us. Henri reminded his readers that the life of Jesus was not merely a series of miraculous deeds of power; it also displayed vulnerability and weakness, as St. Paul had been the first to realize. In his humanity and his suffering Jesus is not far from us, nor was he far from Adam. His life is a model that helps us understand our own humanity, our suffering, and our trials.

Jesus did not come in power and might. He came dressed in weakness. The greatest part of his life was hidden, sharing the human condition of a baby, a young child, a struggling adolescent, and a maturing adult. Adam's hidden life, like the life of Jesus of Nazareth, was an unseen preparation for the time of his ministry to many people, even though neither he nor his parents looked on it that way.

I am not saying that Adam was a second Jesus. But I am saying that because of the vulnerability of Jesus we can see Adam's extremely vulnerable life as a life of utmost spiritual significance. Adam did not have unique heroic virtues: he did not excel at anything that newspapers write about. But I am convinced that Adam was chosen to witness to God's love through his brokenness. To say this is not to romanticize him or to be sentimental. Adam was, like all of us, a limited person, more limited than most, and unable to express himself in words. But he was also a whole person and a blessed man. In his weakness he became a unique instrument of God's grace. He became a revelation of Christ among us.[41]

The Death of Henri Nouwen

Henri lived a remarkable life and announced to the world a compelling message of God's love. It is not surprising that his death was as unique and meaningful as much of his life had been. You could even say that his death is a fitting end to his story. This is how it came about: When Henri's sabbatical came to an end, he returned to the Daybreak community in Canada. He was sixty-four years old, the age when many people retire, but he was still full of plans and energy. Of course, during his absence Henri had been missed. The community celebrated his return in typical l'Arche fashion, and he felt welcomed into the next stage in his life.

"Our life is a short opportunity to say 'yes' to God's love. Our death is a full coming home to that love. Do we desire to come home? It seems that most of our efforts are aimed at delaying this homecoming as long as possible."
—Here and Now

Nouwen's funeral Mass in Utrecht, Holland, September 5, 1996. (Photo by Wendy Crone. Courtesy Photograph Series, Henri Nouwen Archives)

After the funeral Mass in Holland, Henri's brother Laurent and Jean Vanier load his coffin into a hearse to begin his final return to Toronto.
(Courtesy Photograph Series, Henri Nouwen Archives)

"The resurrection doesn't answer any of our curious questions about life after death, such as how will it be? How will it look? But it does reveal to us that, indeed, love is stronger than death. After that revelation, we must remain silent, leave the whys, wheres, hows, and whens behind, and simply trust."

—Our Greatest Gift

Before he settled back down in Canada, there was, however, one more project he needed to attend to. He had agreed to do a film for Dutch television on the theme of the Prodigal Son and on Rembrandt's painting. Part of the movie was to be shot right in the Hermitage in St. Petersburg. So, in the first stage of a necessary trip to Russia, Henri flew to Holland. There he met the film crew and checked into a hotel to rest. Some time after he went upstairs he called down to the desk and requested medical attention. He was not feeling well. Henri was so sick that the fire brigade was called and he was taken out of the room through the window to keep him in a horizontal position. He was then lowered to the street from the rooftop outside. He was rushed to a hospital and examined, and it was quickly determined that he had had a heart attack.

Word went out quickly to Henri's family in Holland and the Daybreak community in Canada. Soon there was a large group of Henri's friends and family gathered in the university town of Hilversum to be with Henri. Nathan Ball arrived from Canada. At first Henri was in terrible pain and unable to speak more than a few words. A priest arrived to hear Henri's confession and administer the last rites. However, he began to get better. At one point he told Nathan, "I don't think I will die, but if I do, please tell everyone that I'm grateful."[42] As he rallied, he was already planning how he would have to cut back and really take things much easier. Those gathered around Henri breathed a sigh of relief. He appeared to be out of immediate danger. In fact, when visiting hours were over, he accompanied Nathan and Jan van den Bosch, the film producer, down in the elevator after saying the night prayers with them.

In hindsight, maybe the hospital staff should have kept Henri under closer observation. That night he suffered another series of heart attacks and he died. In the following days there were two funeral services, the first in Utrecht, and a second in Toronto. Before the services took place in Toronto Henri was placed in a coffin made in the woodshop at Daybreak and decorated with brightly colored drawings by the core members of the community. The holy card handed out at his second funeral had on one side the image of Rembrandt's *Return of the Prodigal Son* and on the other Henri's words, "God is urging me to come home, to enter into his light, and to discover there that, in God, all people are uniquely and completely loved. In the light of God I can finally see my neighbor as my brother, as the one who belongs as much to God as I do."

The parable of the Prodigal Son was not only read at his funeral, but acted out by core members. Henri Nouwen was buried in Canada and, in his memory, his family donated the chalice that Henri had received at his ordination to the Daybreak community. It had originally been given to Henri's uncle Anton, and Henri had written about this same silver chalice in *Can You Drink the Cup?* At the time of his death signed copies of that book were stacked, prepared, and waiting to be mailed to many of his friends. They received this fitting last gift in the weeks after the funeral.

"I do not want to control my own funeral or burial. That's a worry I do not need! But if you want to hear my preference, then I can say this: Keep me away from a funeral home, make a simple wooden coffin in our woodery, let people say goodbye in the Dayspring chapel, and bury me in a plot at Elgin Mills Cemetery where other members of Daybreak can also be buried. And . . . keep it very simple, very prayerful, and very joyful."
—Sabbatical Journey

Henri's second funeral Mass took place in the Slovak Catholic Cathedral of the Transfiguration in Markham, Ontario. (Photo by Mary Carney, used with permission)

A simple wooden cross on Henri's grave in Toronto. (Courtesy Henri Nouwen Literary Centre)

"Thank you, Lord, for every day that you give me to come closer to you. Thank you for your patience and goodness. I pray that when I die I will be at peace. Hear my prayer. Amen."

—A Cry for Mercy

Was he ready to die? It is true that Henri had prepared himself years before for the possibility of his death. Nevertheless, he optimistically expected that he would live to his nineties, like his father. His death came as a profound shock to his community, his friends, his readers, and Christians everywhere. The *National Catholic Reporter's* headline asked openly the question that was in many people's hearts: "Candidate for Sainthood?" The death of someone so vibrant seemed almost impossible, yet it was true.

In fact, the way Henri Nouwen died seems to exhibit God's mercy to an extraordinary degree. Of the many ways he might have died, including dying in Russia or on a transatlantic flight, the way it came about held a great deal of meaning and kindness: His death was in fact a series of "returns." Henri first returned to his community in Canada after a year's absence. Then he returned to Holland, his native land. Before he died he was able to see and say goodbye to his family and to some of his closest friends. Indeed, Nathan Ball was his last visitor. He was in Holland because he was also returning to Rembrandt's magnificent painting, and, by returning to the painting, in the end he returned to God.

Conclusion

It has rightly been said of Henri Nouwen that he lived five or six lives in the space of one. His was not a particularly long life, but as we look at it through even this abbreviated account, it is remarkable how full it was, how many interests he pursued, how many people he reached, how many books he wrote, and how much he accomplished. He lived very intensely. From his days as a seminarian to his last sabbatical and last journey, Henri Nouwen embraced life and lived it deeply.

> *"A flyer must fly, and a catcher must catch, and the flyer must trust, with outstretched arms, that his catcher will be there for him. . . . Dying is trusting in the catcher."*
> —**Our Greatest Gift**

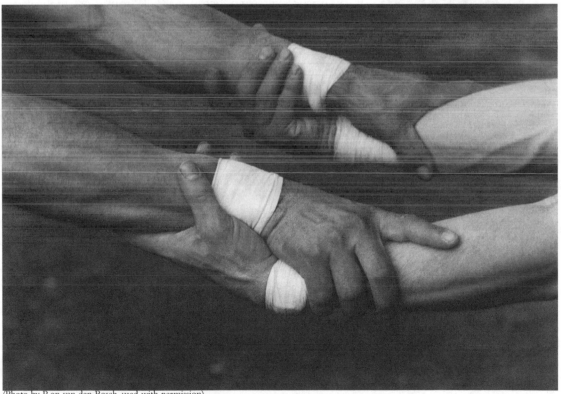

(Photo by Ron van den Bosch, used with permission)

(Courtesy Henri Nouwen Literary Centre)

"My hope is that the description of God's love in my life will give you the freedom and the courage to discover—and maybe also describe— God's love in yours."

—Here and Now

Because of his unique gifts and his boundless enthusiasm and energy, he accomplished an enormous amount. I haven't been able to include here any but the biggest events and themes that were part of his many accomplishments. However, he never allowed the fact that he was so accomplished to affect how he saw himself. His fresh perspective, his creativity, and his humility never failed him. Because of an inborn sense of freedom and because he took himself lightly, he pulled up stakes several times in his life and took off in a completely new direction. Henri was always starting over, and was ever making old things new.

In his last years he became fascinated by the trapeze, and saw it as a metaphor for living in the Spirit. In fact, the trapeze would fit as well or better as a metaphor for his own life. Performing on the trapeze is all about climbing up the rungs of ladders, leaping from safety into thin air, sailing higher and higher toward a great artistic expression, occasional falls from those high places, and coming to rest in the hands of the catcher. Nouwen's instant

(Courtesy Henri Nouwen Literary Centre)

Henri on the beach at Monterey.
(Photo by Peter Weiskel, used with permission)

"When we live our lives as missions, we become aware that there is a home from which we are sent and to which we have to return. We start thinking about ourselves as people who are in a faraway country to bring a message or work on a project, but only for a certain amount of time. When the message has been delivered and the project is finished, we want to return home to give an account of our mission and to rest from our labors."

—Bread for the Journey

affinity with the trapeze could have been due to the fact that his spiritual journey through life was much like a trapeze performance. There was certainly a lot of climbing, a lot of risk taking, a lot of artistry in the heights, and occasional falls. Finally, he came to rest with God, the catcher, as we all do.

God was his constant preoccupation and companion. The most unusual and important thing about Henri Nouwen was how keenly he sought God and his will, and how focused he was on living and spreading the gospel. I have known many priests and many professors of divinity, and yet there are none I can think of who were so earnestly focused on really living in God and living for the gospel as was Henri Nouwen. Henri had many interests, but God always came through at the end of each. Just as the figure of the catcher comes through at the end of his presentations on the trapeze, and the figure of the father comes through at the end of his meditation on Rembrandt's painting, so we see that Henri always found God at the end of his many forays and pursuits.

What else can we say about the life of Henri Nouwen? I

Henri Nouwen's second funeral Mass in Markham, Ontario, on September 28, 1996.
(Copyright: Josko Photograph Studio. Courtesy Photograph Series, Henri Nouwen Archives)

think that we can say that he was very true to himself. He brought a lot of light into the world, but he was only able to do so because he owned up to who he was, accepted his limitations, and took great solace in the friends and family that God had given to him. His psychology background made him very aware of the person, or the self, as the sphere where everything must ultimately come together; thus he was very aware of who he was, and that his life was his responsibility and his opportunity. He restlessly sought to make more of the life he had been given, and it is very interesting to see the evolution of his interests and how he ended his working career at l'Arche. In the end a simpler life with simpler people was richer and more satisfying than Ivy League academia or any of the options he had tried, because God's kingdom is revealed to such as these.

Finally, the life of Henri Nouwen, and the message of Henri Nouwen, must be seen as a gift to the world. Just as he taught us that we all are given to the world, Henri Nouwen was a gift to us, a man whom we could know and love, and who came to us with an impassioned message—that God loves

(Photo by Peter Dwyer, used with permission)

"Is this when his resurrection began, in the midst of my grief? That is what happened to the mourning Mary of Magdala when she heard a familiar voice calling her by her name. That is what happened for the downcast disciples on the road to Emmaus when a stranger talked to them and their hearts burned within them. . . . Mourning turns to dancing, grief turns to joy, despair turns to hope, and fear turns to love. Then hesitantly someone is saying, 'He is risen, he is risen indeed.'"

—Adam

"Suddenly the two disciples, who ate the bread and recognized him, are alone again. But not with the aloneness with which they began their journey. They are alone together, and know that a new bond has been created between them. They no longer look at the ground with downcast faces. They look at each other and say: 'Did not our hearts burn when he talked to us on the road and explained the scriptures to us?'"

—With Burning Hearts

us, each one of us, and that life is an opportunity to say to God, "I love you, too."

Even though I often give in to the many fears and warnings of my world, I still believe deeply that our few years on this earth are part of a much longer event that stretches out far beyond the boundaries of our birth and death. I think of it as a mission into time, a mission that is very exhilarating and even exciting, mostly because the One who sent me on the mission is waiting for me to come home and tell the story of what I have learned.[43]

(Photo by Mary Carney, used with permission)

Notes

[1] Henri Nouwen, *Can You Drink the Cup?* (Notre Dame, IN: Ave Maria, 1996), 15.

[2] Henri Nouwen, *Here and Now, Living in the Spirit* (New York: Crossroad, 1994), 77–78.

[3] Quoted in Michael Ford, *Wounded Prophet: A Portrait of Henri J. M. Nouwen* (New York: Doubleday, 1999), 82.

[4] Henri Nouwen, *Intimacy* (San Francisco: Harper & Row, 1969), 79.

[5] Ibid., 136.

[6] Henri Nouwen, "Anton T. Boisen and Theology through Living Human Documents," *Pastoral Psychology* 19, no. 186 (September 1968): 51.

[7] Seward Hiltner, "Henri Nouwen, Pastoral Theologian of the Year," *Pastoral Psychology,* 27, no. 1 (Fall 1978): 4.

[8] Henri Nouwen, *Reaching Out: The Three Movements of the Spiritual Life* (New York: Doubleday, 1975), 94.

[9] Quoted in Ford, *Wounded Prophet,* 97.

[10] Nouwen, *Intimacy,* 143.

[11] Henri Nouwen, *The Genesee Diary: Report from a Trappist Monastery* (New York: Doubleday, 1976), 68.

[12] Nouwen, *Reaching Out,* 47–48.

[13] Henri Nouwen, *Sabbatical Journey* (New York: Crossroad, 1998), 34.

[14] Ford, *Wounded Prophet,* 29.

[15] Henri Nouwen, in an introduction to Cliff Edwards, *Van Gogh and God* (Chicago: Loyola University, 1989), x.

[16] Nouwen, *The Genesee Diary,* 90–92.

[17] Henri Nouwen, *¡Gracias! A Latin American Journal* (San Francisco: Harper and Row, 1983), xiii–xiv.

[18] Henri Nouwen, foreword to Gustavo Gutiérrez, *We Drink from Our Own Wells* (Maryknoll, NY: Orbis Books, 1984), xv–xvi.

[19] Ibid., xxi.

[20] Henri Nouwen, "My History with God," unpublished manuscript, quoted in Henri Nouwen, *The Road to Peace,* John Dear, ed. (Maryknoll, NY: Orbis Books, 1998) xxii.

[21] Henri Nouwen, *Peacework: Prayer, Resistance, Community* (Maryknoll, NY: Orbis Books, 2005) 76-77

[22] Henri Nouwen, *The Road to Daybreak* (New York: Doubleday, 1988), 22.

[23] Ibid., 11–12.

[24] Henri Nouwen, *Letters to Marc about Jesus* (San Francisco: Harper Collins, 1988), 82.

[25] Mary Bastedo, "Henri and Daybreak: A Story of Mutual Transformation," in Beth Porter, ed., *Befriending Life: Encounters with Henri Nouwen* (New York: Doubleday, 1981), 28.

[26] Nouwen, *The Road to Daybreak,* 220–21.

[27] Henri Nouwen, foreword to The L'Arche Daybreak Community, *Living the Beatitudes: Daily Reflections for Lent* (Cincinnati, OH: St. Anthony Messenger, 1995), 5.

[28] Nouwen, *The Road to Daybreak*, 219–20.

[29] Nouwen, *Road to Daybreak,* 223.

[30] Henri Nouwen, *The Inner Voice of Love* (New York: Doubleday, 1996), 26.

[31] Nouwen, *Can You Drink the Cup?* 72–73.

[32] Nouwen, *Here and Now*, 18.

[33] Henri Nouwen, *The Return of the Prodigal Son* (New York: Doubleday, 1992), 123.

[34] Nouwen, *Sabbatical Journey,* 35.

[35] Henri Nouwen, *Bread for the Journey: A Daybook of Wisdom and Faith* (HarperSanFrancisco: 1997), April 14.

[36] Henri Nouwen, *A Letter of Consolation* (New York: Harper & Row, 1982), 19.

[37] Henri Nouwen, *Beyond the Mirror* (New York: Crossroad, 1990), 35.

[38] Ibid., 72.

[39] Nouwen, *Life of the Beloved* (New York: Crossroad, 1992), 106–7.

[40] Nouwen, *Can You Drink the Cup?,* 25–27.

[41] Henri Nouwen, *Adam: God's Beloved* (Maryknoll, NY: Orbis Books, 1997), 29–30.

[42] Quoted in Ford, *Wounded Prophet,* 202.

[43] Nouwen, *Life of the Beloved,* 110.